Sermons on

Christ's Last Disclosure of Himself

from Revelation 22:16–17

The Spirit and Bride

The Waters of Life

Christ's Free Invitation to Sinners
to Come and Drink of those Waters

by

William Greenhill
(an unworthy servant of the Lord's,
and author of the *Commentary on Ezekiel*)

Edited by Rev. Don Kistler

Soli Deo Gloria Publications
. . . for instruction in righteousness . . .

Soli Deo Gloria Publications
P.O. Box 451, Morgan, PA 15064
(412) 221-1901/FAX 221-1902

*

*

ISBN 1-57358-104-6

*

Contents

The Epistle Dedicatory

To my dearly beloved brethren and fellow members of that body, the church at Stepney, of which Christ is the Head, grace, mercy, and peace from God our Father, and Jesus Christ our Lord, be multiplied unto you.

Brethren:

You are here presented with that in print which before you have heard preached unto you; but I hope the impression of it is not only in these papers, but that it is already in your hearts. It was a glorious commendation that Paul gave of his Corinthians: "Ye are our epistle written in our hearts, known and read of all men, forasmuch as ye are manifestly declared to be the epistle of Christ ministered by us, written not with ink, but with the Spirit of the living God, not in tables of stone, but in fleshly tables of the heart" (2 Corinthians 3:2–3).

What is the end of our faithful pastors' preaching, and of your hearing, but that we may be epistles of Christ?

You have here presented to your view some of the last words of Christ, wherein you have a declaration of what He is, the root and offspring of David—David's root in regard to His deity and his offspring in regard to His humanity. We need to hear these truths again and again, especially in such days of apostasy and falling away from the faith as we live in. Many deny the Lord who bought them, by which we may see the Scripture fulfilled which says that in the last days many shall depart from the faith. In 2 Peter 2:1–2, the apostle plainly says that as there were false prophets of old, so there will be false teachers who will creep in, bringing damnable heresies, "even denying the Lord that bought them; and many shall follow their pernicious ways, by reason of whom the way of truth shall be evil spoken of."

You have here, likewise, a sweet and blessed invitation of the Lord Jesus to poor, thirsty sinners that they would come and take of the water of life freely. Oh, therefore, let us not stand off, but come, even though we have no money, for little do we think what prejudice our souls receive because we do not go more freely to Jesus Christ to receive the things that He has purchased, and is ready to give to us. You are called out of the world, even to obtain the glory of our Lord Jesus Christ.

You are members of Christ (1 Corinthians 6:15). "Ye are the temple of the Holy Spirit" (1 Corinthians 6:19). You stand in near relation to God and Christ, as His friends, His jewels, His peculiar treasure, His vineyard, His pleasant plant, His glory. You are a chosen generation, a royal priesthood, a holy nation, a peculiar people (1 Peter 2:9).

It being so, what flows from here, or what does this call for at our hands, but that we labor to show forth the praises of Him who has called us out of darkness into His marvelous light? Therefore, let us not walk after our own lusts, but in the fear of God, as the churches did in Acts 9:31. You are the children of the light (1 Thessalonians 5:5); therefore, let us walk in the light. You have a spiritual life begotten in you who were once dead; "therefore let us walk in newness of life" (Romans 6:4). Let us walk in and after the Spirit

(Galatians 5:16), in good works (Ephesians 2:10), in love (Ephesians 5:2), circumspectly (Ephesians 5:15). Yea, let us walk honestly towards those who are outside the body of Christ (1 Thessalonians 4:12). Let us walk in the truth (3 John 4). Let us walk in the steps of good men (Proverbs 2:20). Yea, let us walk even as Christ Himself walked (1 John 2:6).

And that we may do so, let us mind our rule (Galatians 6:16), and then we shall walk in some measure worthy of our vocation (Ephesians 4:1). This will make much for the glory of God and Christ here in this world; by it we shall adorn the doctrine of God our Savior (Titus 2:10). It will make much for the comfort and joy of him whom God has set over us, who watches for our souls. Yea, your holy walking and godly conduct may be a means for the conversion of others, and bringing them into Jesus Christ (1 Peter 2:12 and 3:1–2). And by doing this, we shall not only maintain our fellowship one with another, but with the Father and the Son (1 John 1:3).

Beloved brethren, I shall not need to put you on to the ready entertaining of these choice truths that are here delivered, as they are already written in your hearts. You cannot but receive them with joy, and in so doing you answer the end and labors of him who is dear unto you, who preached them, and, likewise, the end of him who transcribed them.

Brethren, farewell; be perfect; be of good comfort; be of one mind; live in peace, and the God of love and peace shall be with you. So prays your dear brother, who affectionately loves you and is desirous to serve you in the Lord,

William Greenhill

To the Reader

That these sermons see the light is more the result of the labors of their hearers than of the author. Some, being affected in hearing them, were importunate to have them published, urging that they might be of use not only to doubting saints and despondent Christians, but also to those who were dead in sins and trespasses. Hereupon, after some strugglings in my spirit, I was willing to expose myself to censure rather than to grieve my friends by a denial and withhold those truths by which possibly some poor soul might gain some little spiritual advantage.

Reader, although these sermons were taken by the pen of a ready writer, and printed as they were taken, yet do not look for that spirit, power, and life that was in them when they were preached. The press is a dead thing compared to the pulpit. A sermon from the pulpit is like meat from the fire, like milk from the breast; but when it is on paper, it is only cold meat and milk, and has lost its lively taste, though it may nourish and become a standing dish to feed upon. This is the benefit in printing: when the preacher is absent or dead, the printed thing may be at hand and serviceable.

Reader, if you look for high notions, quaint expressions, new opinions, strong lines, enticing words of man's wisdom, or anything to please a fleshly mind, I must say to you as Peter did to that man in the book of Acts, "Such silver and gold have I none; but what I have I give unto thee," and that is plain and naked truths, according to the simplicity of Christ and the gospel.

Would you know what is to be had here? If you are shaken in these staggering times, here you may see what a root Christ is, bearing all up. If you stumble at Christ's meanness in the world, here you shall understand of what royal descent He was. If you are in the dark and do not know the right way, here you may behold Christ, a glorious star to direct you. If you are dull and sad, here you may hear the sweet voices of the Spirit and Bride to quicken and comfort you. If you are thirsty, here is water, water of life prepared for you. If you are sinful, and so sinful as to fear that Christ will not save you, here you shall find many clear demonstrations of how willing Christ is to save sinners. If you find no willingness in you to have water of life, here is revealed how that willingness may be wrought in you. If you are secure and sleepy, here are tidings of Christ's coming, of what concern that is, and what preparation you are to make for it which may help to awaken you.

In a word, here you have the last discovery the Lord Christ gave forth of Himself and of His mind. He had often before revealed what He was: the Messiah (John 4:25–26), the resurrection and the life (John 11:25), the bread of life (John 6:35), the light of the world (John 8:12), the good shepherd (John 10:11), the true vine (John 15:1), the way, the truth, and the life (John 14:6), and the Alpha and Omega. Here He said, "I am the Root and Offspring of David." This, being the last declaration of Himself, doubtless has something considerable in it, as will appear in the work itself.

William Greenhill

Christic the Root of All

"I am the Root, and the Offspring of David."
Revelation 22:16

Christ, having sent His angel to testify several things unto the churches, tells them what He is: "I am the Root and the Offspring of David, the Bright and Morning Star." These words ("I am the Root and the offspring of David") are a riddle and a seeming contradiction. For Christ to be the Root of David and the offspring of David seems very improbable and contradictory, much like that speech in Matthew 22 where Christ said, " 'The Lord said unto my Lord . . .' If David calls Him 'Lord,' how is He then His Son?" They could not tell what to make of it. So it is probable that when many read these words, that Christ is both the Root and Offspring of David, they do not know how to untie this knot and to reconcile this seeming contradiction. But if we plow with the heifer of the Lord, with His Spirit, we may easily resolve it.

Christ is the Root of David as He is God in His human nature. He is the Offspring of David as He is man. And in some sense Christ, as He is man, may also be the Root of David; for Christ's human nature was in Jesse, the father of David, as well as in David himself.

You see here that Christ is called a root. "I am the Root of David." Of that I shall speak at this time; and it is not in vain that the Scripture sets Christ out by this expression of a root, for there are sundry resemblances wherein the Lord Christ is like a root.

1

First, a root is a thing that is hidden in the earth, secret, and not obvious to the eye. So if you especially take the Lord Christ in His divine nature, that is a hidden thing. It is said that God is the invisible God, and Christ's divine nature is an invisible nature. The angels are not seen; souls are not seen; God is not seen; and the deity of Christ is not seen. It was hidden under flesh, under His human nature. And Christ's human nature, Christ as man, was a hidden thing. John 1:10: "He was in the world, and the world was made by Him, and the world knew Him not." The world did not know Him to be the Messiah, to be the root of David. So John 16:3: "These things will they do unto you because they have not known the Father, nor Me." Christ was not known, but was a hidden thing, a secret thing, like a root in the earth. He said of the Spirit in John 14:17: "Whom the world cannot receive because it seeth Him not, neither knoweth Him." The world did not see the Spirit, nor know the Spirit; so the world did not see Christ, nor know Christ. Why, Christ's human nature, Christ as man, was hidden under afflictions, under reproaches, under poverty and meanness, under scorn and contempt, so that He was a root in the earth; He was a hidden thing.

Second, a root has life in it; and the life is principally in the root of anything. So in the Lord Jesus there is life, and life principally in Him. John 5:26: "As the Father hath life in Himself, so hath He given to the Son to have life in Himself." Christ has life in Himself principally and eminently, as the Father had. John 1:4: "In Him was life, and that life was the light of men." In this Root was life; in Christ was life (1 Corinthians 15). He is said to be a quickening Spirit. He has life in Himself, and quickens others. John 14:6 says that He is "the life." He is life emphatically above all others. He is a Root, having life principally and eminently in Himself.

Third, the root, bears up the tree, the branches, and the fruit of the tree; it bears up all. "Thou bearest not the root, but the root bears thee" (Romans 11:18). So it is the Lord Jesus Christ, this Root, who bears up all.

Christ bears up the world. Christ bears up the Church. Christ bears up heaven. He bears up all. Hebrews 1:3: "Upholding all things by the word of His power." The Lord Jesus is the Root, I say, that bears and upholds the whole creation. Zion itself and heaven itself are upheld by this Root, but especially the Church in this world—especially Zion, and the members of Zion, believing souls. John 15:5: "I am the vine"; that is, "I am the Root of the vine." The Church is the vine, and Christ is its root, and He bears up the whole vine, and all the branches, and all the clusters upon the vine. He bears them up. He is the Root of the vine, so that Christ is a Root who bears up all. He bore up David, David's family, and David's kingdom. He bears up Zion, and all the children of Zion.

Fourth, the root conveys life, sap, and nourishment unto the whole body, to all the branches. So it is the Lord Jesus Christ who conveys sap, life, and nourishment unto all His body. Every branch in the vine receives the virtue from the root of the vine; and all have life from Christ. "I am come that ye may have life" (John 10:10). All life is from Christ, and all light is from Christ. He is "the Morning Star." All nourishment is from Christ. He is said to be the Head of the Church, and the Head of the Church is the Root of the Church in the scriptural sense.

And from the Head is all influence of light, direction, counsel, motion, and comfort; all is from the Head; all is from this Root.

From Christ all is conveyed. "Without Me, ye can do nothing. Unless you are in Me, and have virtue from Me, and derive all from Me, you can do nothing."

Thus you see that Christ is a root, the Root of David.

But there are some disparities, or things wherein Christ is not like a root.

First, a root (take it in a literal sense, the roots of trees and plants) is of a dying, decaying nature, and will grow rotten and die. Job 14:8: "Though the root thereof wax old in the earth, and the stock thereof die in the ground." The root of a tree waxes old, and will die and perish and come to nothing; but Christ is not like a root in that sense, for Christ lives forever (Hebrews 7). This Root never dies, never decays. Christ is the same yesterday, the same today, the same tomorrow, and the same forever. He is the Root of Zion forever, and the Root of David forever.

Second, a root bears but one tree; it suffices to uphold one or two or three bodies at most. The root of a stalk of corn will perhaps suffice for two or three, or even for half a dozen stalks; but it cannot suffice for all. But Christ is a root that suffices for all: for all Zion, for the whole world, for the Church, for heaven. He is the Root of David, the Root of Jesse, the Root of Abraham and of Isaac. He is the Root of all the prophets, all the apostles, and all believers, of all who have spiritual life in them; He is the Root of them all. So this Root is of another nature than those roots.

Third, other roots are subject to the wills, humors, and pleasures of men. Men can dig up the roots of things; they can burn and abuse the roots; but Christ is not subject to the wills or dispositions of any, to be spoiled or consumed. The scribes and Pharisees thought to root out this Root when they put Him to death; but when He was in the grave He saw no corruption. He laid down His life, and no one took it from Him without His permission. And He rose again (Romans 1:4), and mightily declared Himself to be the Son of God by the Spirit of holiness. He declared Himself to be a Root that man has no power over.

OBJECTION. "You say that Christ is the Root of David, and the Root of all. Why, did Christ have no root Himself? Was He not from a root, and how then can He be the root of all? Isaiah 11:1: 'And there shall come forth a Rod out of the stem of Jesse, and a Branch shall grow out of his roots.' This means that Christ would come out of Jesse, and Jesse would be the root of Christ. And verse 10 says that 'in that day there shall be a Root of Jesse, which shall stand for an ensign of the people.' The same is said to be the Root of Jesse which is said to be the stem or branch of Jesse. How are these things to be resolved?"

ANSWER. As I answered before, Jesse is the root of Christ according to His human nature, and Christ is the Root of Jesse according to His divine nature. Or, if you will, Christ as Mediator was the Root of Jesse, and of all the godly.

The text now explained, I shall give you this observation on the words "I am the Root of Jesse."

OBSERVATION: The Lord Christ is the Root of nature, the Root of grace, and the Root of glory.

How will this appear? Why, He was the Root of David as a man, the Root of David as a saint, and the Root of

David as glorified. David was now in heaven.

He was the Root of David as a man. Psalm 119:73: "Thy hands have made me and fashioned me, O Lord." David said, "I did not make myself, and my parents did not make me, but Thy hands have made me and fashioned me. Thy hand hath made me such a creature; Thy hand curiously worked on me when I was in my mother's womb; Thy hand framed me, molded me, ordered all my bones and sinews and joints and parts and faculties, and the like. Thy hand hath made me." The work of nature was from Him, so that He was the Root of nature.

And so likewise He was the Root of grace and the Root of glory. David said in Psalm 110, "The Lord said unto my Lord . . . ." How was Christ David's Lord? Because He had given him grace and made him His servant; because He would give him glory. "The Lord said unto my Lord, 'Sit thou at My right hand.' " Christ was David's Lord because He gave him grace, and would later give him glory. Hence it is that he says in Psalm 84:11, "Grace and glory will He give, and no good thing will He withhold." "Well, I have grace, and I shall have more grace. I have a human glory, as I am a king and a prophet, and shall have greater glory. I shall have glory in the highest heavens." So you see that it is true of David that Christ is the Root of his nature, the Root of his grace, and the Root of his glory.

Now it will appear generally that He is the Root of nature, grace, and glory.

First, it will appear that *Christ is the Root of nature* from the creation and making of all things. He who makes all things must be the Lord, the Root, the Author, and the Fountain of nature. Hebrews 1:2: "By whom also He made the world." Why, the world was made by Christ, by His right hand. Christ's arm was at work in the making of all the creatures. The world was made by Him; therefore He is the Lord of nature who has made all.

Second, it appears that He is the root of nature because He can blast nature at His pleasure. What did Christ say to the fig tree? "Never may fruit grow more upon this tree." Did it not immediately wither away? Christ dried up all the moisture, dried up the sap, dried up the very root of the tree. Therefore, He is the very Root, and the Lord of nature.

Third, it further appears in regard that He has command of all diseases. He cured and healed them. What disease was ever presented to Christ that He could not cure? He cast out devils, cured leprosies and all manner of diseases: the woman who had spent all her estate with physicians and could do no good, the man who lay at the pool of Bethesda and could not be cured. Christ cures all diseases. He is the Root of nature.

Fourth, it also appears from His raising the dead. When men are on the verge of dissolution, and nature is going downward—the breath is gone, the soul is gone, the body is putrefied—it does not matter to Christ. He said to Martha, "Thou shalt see the glory of God." In other words, "You shall see that I am the Root of nature; that I am the Root of all; that I can call the soul, breathe back into him, and raise him up." These are evidences that He is the Root and Lord of nature.

Christ is the Root of grace. All grace is from Him. Luke 4:18: "The Spirit of the Lord is upon Me, because He hath anointed Me to preach the gospel, to preach it to the poor. He hath sent Me to heal the brokenhearted, to preach deliverance to the captives and recovering of

sight to the blind, to set at liberty them that are
bruised, to preach the acceptable year of the Lord." Is
there not grace in all these? Yes, and all comes from
Christ. He was anointed with the Spirit of the Lord to
do these things. This is given to us even more fully in
John 1:14–17: "The Word was made flesh, and dwelt
among us, full of grace and truth." But for whom was
this grace, and for whom was this truth? John says,
"And of His fullness have we all received, and grace for
grace." He had a fullness of grace. He was the Author,
the Root of grace, the Fountain of grace, the God of
grace; and this grace was to be communicated and derived unto others. "Of His fullness have we all received,
grace for grace. For the law was given by Moses, but
grace and truth came by Jesus Christ."

The Lord Christ is the Root of grace. Romans 5:20–
21: "Where sin abounded, grace did much more
abound, that as sin hath reigned unto death, even so
might grace reign through righteousness unto eternal
life by Jesus Christ our Lord." Sin abounded, aye, but
grace superabounds. How does it come to super-
abound? "By Jesus Christ our Lord." Grace must reign
as sin has reigned, and it must reign by Christ. This
grace will send out so much grace that grace will reign,
and outreign sin; it will bring sin under. So, then,
Christ is the Root of grace.

Lastly, *Christ is the Root of glory.* There is no one who is
let into heaven but by Christ; none is made glorious but
by Christ. 1 Corinthians 2:8 says that "they crucified the
Lord of glory." He is called there "the Lord of glory."

He is the Lord of glory because He was a glorious
Lord in Himself. He is the Lord of glory because He
has all glory to dispose of, because He advances whom

He pleases to glory. He will advance His Church unto glory, all believers unto glory. So now you see that Christ is the Root of nature, the Root of grace, and the Root of glory.

Application

Now what remains but that we should make some use of this point; and there are several things which will be observable.

USE 1. First, if Christ is the Root of nature, of grace, and of glory, then we may all make use of that which David did upon this account. Psalm 138:8: "Thy mercy, O Lord, endures forever; forsake not the works of Thine own hands."

Why, may not everyone say, "Lord, I am the work of Thy hands. Thou hast made me a creature. Thou art the Root of my nature. Lord, do not forsake me, but, Lord, make me gracious as well as to have nature. Be the Root not only of a natural life to me, but the Root of a spiritual life unto me, the Root of glory unto me. Thy hand hath made me. Thou hast made me a man, given me an immortal soul, and endued me with understanding, and some wisdom and knowledge. Lord, do not forsake me; leave me not to the devil, to the world, or to myself. But, Lord, since Thy hand hath made me a man, let it make me a new man. As I have a natural life, so let me have another life, a spiritual life."

When anyone is in trials and troubles, in difficulties and afflictions, and thinks he has been left by God and Christ, let him use this argument in prayer: "I am the work of Thine hands. What, wilt Thou leave the work of Thy own hands? Men will not desert the work of their

own hands. Thou hast not deserted the creation: the
sun, moon, stars, night, day, summer and winter. Why,
Lord, I am the work of Thine own hands. Do not leave
me nor forsake me."

USE 2. Is Christ the Root of nature, of grace, and of
glory? Then whatever difference you see in men as
men, in men as Christians, whatever difference you
read of men in glory, is all from the Lord Jesus Christ;
it is from the Root. You know that one tree is higher
than another; that is from the root. One tree or branch
is higher or bigger than another; that is from the root
of the tree. The differences are in the branches, arms,
and boughs of the tree; and that is all from the root of
that tree. So the differences that are among men are
from the root. Christ gives to one man great parts, to
another man lesser parts. He gives to one man a strong
judgment, a strong memory, admirable elocution; and
to another man He does not give the same. The difference is in Christ. He is the Root of nature, and com-
municates what He pleases.

So it is likewise with the talents of grace. He gives to
one man one talent, to another man two talents, and to
another man five talents. The Lord is the Root, and He
makes one higher than another. Some men have
choice gifts and graces; some man has more than ten
other men have. It may be that one man is beneath him
in a degree or two; some are beneath him by a great
deal. In grace some are babes, some children, some
young men, and some old disciples.

So it is in glory. The twelve apostles shall sit upon
twelve thrones. In glory some are like the sun, some
like the moon, and some like the stars. What is the
difference? The difference lies in the Root: He com-

municates what He pleases in natural matters, in spiritual matters, and in glory.

USE 3. If Christ is the Root, then let us not be highminded; let none be lifted up with whatever enjoyments they have. Whatever gifts you have, whatever graces you have, whatever glory you look for, do not be lifted up. The reason is plain, and so Romans 11:18 says, "Boast not against the branches." Why, another man is a branch as well as you are. Take man as man: he is a branch of the tree of nature. And will you boast in yourself against him? Boast not of your wit, beauty, strength, or any natural abilities you have; for you do not bear the Root, but the Root bears you.

So do not boast of spiritual matters, that you have so much faith, so much knowledge, so much patience, humility, and love; do not boast of these things. Christ is the Root, and the Root bears you.

Do not boast of what places you shall have in heaven. The sons of Zebedee wanted to be at the right and left hands of Christ when they came into His kingdom. They wanted to have such and such places. But know that the Root bears you. Be humble and lowly therefore; what you have, you have received. Why are you then lifted up as if you had not received it? The Root, the Lord Christ, will call you to an account one day of what you have received, and how you have employed it. Therefore, remember that you have all from the Root, and nothing of your own.

USE 4. If Christ is the Root that bears all up, the Root of nature, grace, and glory, then let us fear to offend and provoke Him. If a man's life, habitation, and maintenance depended upon one man, would he not take heed how he provoked that man? Does not your all

depend upon this Root, Christ? Does not your nature
depend upon Him? In Him you live and move and have
your being; your habitation and maintenance depend
upon Him.

With regard to your spiritual life and spiritual good,
do they not depend on this Root? Is He not the Root of
life, of all spiritual life, comfort, and blessings? Is He
not the Root from whom you receive all grace, all truth,
and all comforts and good?

Do you not look, through Him, to have your glory?
Why will you offend Him now and sin against Him?
Oh, what a root is this that bears up all nature, that
bears up all grace, that bears up all glory, and bears up
all the spiritual good of men and women—the root that
bears up heaven and glory! Take heed, I say, of tram-
pling upon this root, of wronging Christ, of slighting
Christ, of grieving Christ, of displeasing Him in any
way. If He withdraws the influences of nature, you must
die immediately. If He withdraws the influences of
grace, you must sit in darkness immediately. If He
should withdraw glory from you, where would you be
but outside the doors?

USE 5. Again, if Christ is the Root of nature, grace,
and glory, then let us make it our business to serve and
honor Him. Is it not the duty of a child, coming from
the loins of his parents, to serve and honor them? So it
is the duty of every man, seeing that Christ is the Root
of every man, to serve the Lord. Serve Him with your
eyes, with your tongue, with your hand, with your foot;
serve Him with your understanding; serve Him with
your will; serve Him with your affections; serve Him
with the whole man, for you have all from Him, as a
man, and so you should let all then return to Him.

Waters that come from the sea run back again to the sea. And, seeing that we all come from Christ, who is God and the Root of nature, let us then work properly and serve Him.

But much more is this true of you who are spiritual. Has Christ given you life, spiritual life, and quickened you when you were dead in your trespasses and sins? Is Christ the Root of all your spiritual good and welfare? Will you not serve Christ? What, will you be for the world, for hell, and for sin now? Why, Christ is your Root; are you then His vine, and will you not live for Christ? Certainly we should serve and honor Christ upon this account. And we would do it if we considered, "Why, I have my life of faith, of grace, and of comfort; and I hope for glory hereafter from Christ. And shall I not serve the Lord Jesus Christ? I look for glory; therefore I will purify myself as He is pure."

Christ in you is the hope of glory. Is He your Root, and have you hope of glory? Then purify yourselves as He is pure; yea, serve Christ with pure hearts, pure affections, and pure conduct. Live to the Lord Jesus. He is the Root of nature, the Root of spiritual life, and the Root of glory.

USE 6. Again, if Christ is the Root of all, then here you may know what your conditions are, what state you are in. Tell me what root you are rooted in, what root you grow on. Do you grow upon the old Adam still, or are you rooted in Christ? If old Adam is your root, as he is the root of mankind, of corrupt man, then if you grow upon that root you are no more than when you came into the world. Your fruit is sour; your grapes are wild grapes; your natures are corrupt; you are enemies to God; and you are upon the root of bitterness, which is a root of death.

Nay, let me say this: Are you in Christ now, since He alone is God? For Christ is the Root of nature, as He is God. If you are rooted in Christ, because He has made you, but if you are no more than this, you have marred yourselves since He made you. Therefore, make inquiry whether you are rooted upon Christ as Mediator, as the Root of David, as the God-man; ask whether you have an interest in Christ upon that account. And if such is the case, your fruit is good fruit, fruit becoming the gospel, fruit worthy of grace, and worthy of a man who is called justified and sanctified. Now you bear other fruit, such fruit as Christ bore. Those who are translated, cut off from the old Adam and engrafted into Christ, bear other fruit than before. Therefore, inquire what root you are in, whether you are rooted in Christ, yes or no. That will yield a great deal of comfort to you if it is so.

USE 7. If Christ is the Root of nature, the Root of grace, the Root of glory, and the Root of all, then this is a great comfort unto every true Christian. That person is planted in Christ and shall never dry up or wither away. In Psalm 1, the psalmist speaks of a tree, planted beside the water, that brings forth fruit in its season. His leaf also will not wither. Why, he who is a true Christian, who is intrinsically engrafted into Christ, is such a root as has life, water of life, and virtue, and is communicating continually unto the branches. "I am come that ye may have life, and that ye may have it more abundantly" (John 10:10). If you are truly in Christ, you shall have life, and have it more abundantly. You are in a river of water; you are in a Root who has an abundance of all spiritual good and spiritual blessings for you. Therefore, look to it that you are in Christ, and then you shall have virtue in Him; your root shall never wither, and it shall never decay.

USE 8. If Christ is the Root of all, then be exhorted, every one of you, to get an interest in this Root. Get an interest in Him, and then your natures will be sanctified; get an interest in Him, and then you will have of all the fullness of Christ, and you shall have of all His glory. Men and women labor to be rooted in the world, to be rooted in sin. Oh, how men are rooted in sin, rooted in wicked practices! How they are rooted in worldly things, and so entangled and fixed that there is no getting them off or out of the world! What phrase does the apostle use in Colossians 2:7?—"rooted and built up in Christ." But where? In Christ; it is good to be rooted in Christ. Oh, labor to be rooted in Him, rooted in the love of Christ, in the power of Christ, in the merits of Christ, in the intercession of Christ. Oh, labor to be rooted in these, and then you will grow.

And the way to be rooted in these is really twofold. There are but two principal things that I shall name: the first is by faith and the second is by love.

Get faith in Christ. That unites you to Him; and the more faith, the more rooted you are in Him. Get farther and farther into Christ; labor for faith, and that will fix you, settle you, and establish you in Christ. It is our lack of faith that makes us be off and on with God and with Christ, and such poor creatures as we are. Well, labor for faith, and that is a drawing virtue, a drawing grace; it will draw from Christ whatever is to be had in Him.

And then love the Lord Jesus. Where there is love, how it roots a man in the heart of a man or woman. So if you love the Lord Jesus more, you will be rooted more in Him. This is the way to be rooted in Christ: get faith and get love.

USE 9. If Christ is the Root of reason, the Root of grace and glory, the Root of all, then let us give the glory and praise of all to Jesus Christ and attribute nothing to ourselves or others. We are wonderfully apt, when we see a tree full of fruit, to attribute it to the tree. "Oh, there is a very good tree." You do not look to the root; you attribute nothing to that, whereas it is the root that you should attribute it to. So, now, we attribute to ourselves our own endeavors, labors, improvements and diligence; but we do not look at the Root. We do not look at Christ, who is the Root of nature. We do not look at Christ who is the Root of grace. We do not look at Christ who is the Root of glory.

Therefore, see the reason why we are so little in thankfulness: we have so little faith. But if we had more faith now to see the Root, we would be more thankful. The root is a hidden thing, as I said before. Christ is in heaven, and Christ's divine nature was hidden; and because we do not see Christ as God, because we do not see Christ as Mediator, because we do not look at Christ as all in all, therefore we do not give that glory to Him, but we look at second causes, means, ordinances, magistrates, parents, friends, and the like. And so God and Christ lose their glory and their honor. But if you would look at the Root, and say, "Oh, this comes from Christ; this comes from God; this comes from the Mediator, from His grace. Yes, all comes from Him"—oh, then, your heart would be carried out to speak of and glorify His name!

Well, look at Christ, for you have nothing that is not from Him. Therefore, not to me, nor to others, but "unto Thee alone, O Lord, be all the glory!"

Christ's Royal Descent

"And the Offspring of David." Revelation 22:16

I now proceed to the next words: "the Offspring of David." The word for "offspring" signifies that from whence another thing comes or proceeds. In Philippians 3:5 Paul speaks of being circumcised on the eighth day, and being of the stock or offspring of Israel. He said he was of the Israelites, that he proceeded and came from them. He was of that race and generation. Isaiah 44:3: "I will pour water upon him that is thirsty, and floods upon dry ground. I will pour My Spirit upon thy seed, and My blessing upon thine offspring"; that is, upon those who are of thy loins and who descend from thee. That is the meaning of the word "offspring": your children are your offspring. So the meaning here is that the Lord Jesus Christ is of the race of David. In the Scriptures He is said to be the seed of the woman (Genesis 3). He is said to be the Son of Abraham (Matthew 1), and the Offspring of David here. He is of the race of mankind, of the race of David.

In Matthew 1:1 we read: "The book of the generation of Jesus Christ, the Son of David." And Christ is frequently called "the Son of David" in the gospels. Matthew 9:27: "Thou, Son of David, have mercy on us."

Now, to open the words yet a little farther, let me pose a question.

QUESTION. Why is Christ said to be the Offspring of David rather than of any other person, when in Matthew 1 He is the Offspring of all mentioned there?

ANSWER. There are several reasons for it:

1. David was he who founded the kingdom of Israel, and there began the foundation of that kingdom. Saul was the first king, but Saul gave way to wrath and was rejected by God. Therefore it is not called the kingdom of Saul, and the reckoning is not from Saul, but it is called the kingdom of David, and the reckoning is from David. David was a most eminent and well-known person in Israel, of great reputation. 2 Chronicles 13:5: "Ought ye not to know that the Lord God of Israel gave the kingdom over Israel to David our father forever, even to him and to his sons by a covenant of salt?" God gave the kingdom to David, and David was the most eminent king and founder of the kingdom of Israel. Therefore David is mentioned here rather than someone else. Christ is the Offspring of David, who was the founder of the kingdom of Israel.

2. David was the most lively type of Jesus Christ of anyone in the entire Scriptures, and therefore Christ is named the Offspring of David rather than any other. David was beloved of God, and so his name signifies. David, you know, slew the bear and the lion, protecting the sheep and the lamb from them. David killed Goliath and freed the whole army of Israel from him. David was a great warrior and a great conqueror, and won famous victories. David brought back the ark of God. David endured great afflictions after he was anointed king, and for many years before he came to the throne and the kingdom also. David likewise was a prophet, and in Psalm 22 David is set out fully as a type of Christ all throughout that psalm.

So Christ was the Beloved of God. And Christ delivered the lambs from the bear and the lion. Christ slew

Goliath in that He led captivity captive. The Lord Christ obtained great victories over the world, sin, Satan, and all our spiritual enemies. The Lord Christ brought back the ark, the truths of God that were in darkness and hidden. He brought immortality and life to light again.

The Lord endured a great deal of misery in this world before He went to glory; and therefore He is said to be the Offspring of David rather than anyone else.

3. But, lastly, it is because the prophecy was that Messiah would be the Son of David. God had promised David that out of his loins Christ would come. 2 Samuel 7:15–16: "But My mercy shall not depart away from him, as I took it from Saul, whom I put away before thee. And thine house and thy kingdom shall be established forever before thee; thy throne shall be established forever." Mark it, God promises him a throne that would be established forever. He must have a seed then, and about that God swears unto him. Psalm 89:35–36: "Once have I sworn by My holiness that I will not lie unto David. His seed shall endure forever, and his throne as the sun before Me." This is spoken of Christ the Seed; and the Scripture says that of the seed of David Messiah would come.

Though the promise was made to Abraham that Christ would come of his seed, and He is said to be the Son of Abraham, yet David is put first because the promise was made later to David than to Abraham. Therefore the eyes of the Jews were upon that promise rather than any other. Hence you find that it was ordinary and common for them to look at Christ as the Son of David. Matthew 15:22: "A woman of Canaan came out of the same coast, and cried unto Him, saying, 'Have

mercy upon me, O Lord, Thou Son of David.' " And
Matthew 20:30: "And behold, two blind men sitting by
the wayside, when they heard that Jesus passed by, cried
out, saying, 'Have mercy on us, O Lord, Thou Son of
David.' " And Matthew 21:9: "And the multitudes that
went before, and that followed after, cried, saying,
'Hosanna to the Son of David.' " Even all sorts looked
at the Messiah to be the Son of David and the Offspring
of David. Hence it is that David is named here rather
than others.

OBJECTION. Isaiah 53:8 says, "And who shall declare His generation?" If Christ is the Son of David, everyone may declare His generation. Therefore, how do
the Scriptures correspond? Isaiah asks, "Who shall declare His generation?" and Matthew and John tell His
generation; they tell that He is the Son of David and the
Offspring of David.

ANSWER. First of all, know that some expositors,
and that not without cause, refer this verse in Isaiah to
Christ's divine nature and generation of God. So when
Isaiah writes, "Who shall declare His generation?" he
means, "Who can declare how the Father begat the
Son?" Whoever can declare how Christ, from all eternity, should be a Son, let that man arise and set his gifts
and graces to work to the uttermost he can, and show
the generation of Christ, His eternal generation. It is
beyond the comprehension of men or angels; therefore, I say, some expositors refer to that, and so ask,
"Who can tell His generation?"

It may be referring to the days and years that Christ
was to live and continue after His incarnation; for he
speaks in this chapter of Christ as suffering as man.
"Who shall declare His generation? For He was cut off

out of the land of the living; who shall declare His generation?" That is, "Who shall declare the continuance of His days and time?" For they thought that when He was cut off, there had been an end of His days. But there was no end to Christ's days, for though His human nature was laid in the grave, yet there was a root underneath that one, the divine nature; and He was raised again and lives forever (Hebrews 7). Revelation 1:18: "I am He that liveth and was dead, and behold, I am alive forevermore." Who shall declare His generation?—that is, who shall declare the days and years that Christ now shall live? He lives forever; He lives forevermore. Who shall declare His generation?

I think the best explanation is that "Who shall declare His generation?" refers to the offspring which shall come from Him; for we say that the generation of such a man is his posterity. "Who shall declare His generation?"—that is, who shall declare His seed, His children, those who shall be His? For the Lord Christ has a seed. Hebrews 2:13: "Behold, I and the children which Thou hast given Me." Christ had children; He had an offspring. In Isaiah 9:6 He is called "the Everlasting Father" because He has children, children in all ages and in all generations. Acts 21:20: "Thou seest, brother, how many thousands of Jews there are which believe." How many "ten thousands," as the word signifies in the original; how many millions? And in Revelation 7, there was sealed out of every tribe twelve thousand, which comes to one hundred forty-four thousand. Verse 9: "After this I beheld, and, lo, a great multitude which no man could number, of all nations." So the Lord Jesus Christ has a seed; He has a generation, a posterity that cannot be numbered, a generation that cannot be declared as to how many they are. So this hinders nothing, nor contradicts what is delivered here: that Christ is the Offspring of David.

The words being thus opened, I shall draw forth some conclusions from them.

OBSERVATION 1. If Jesus Christ is the Offspring of David, then Christ was and is true man. This is, or ought to be, an article of your faith. The offspring of anything is of the same nature as the thing from whence it comes. The offspring of a tree is of the same nature as the tree. So now, if Christ is the Offspring of David, He must be of the same nature as David; else He could not be his Offspring. If David, therefore, was a true man with flesh and blood and spirit and bones, so must the Lord Jesus Christ be of the same nature with him.

Some have denied that Christ was man, just as some have denied that He was God; but He was the Offspring of David. And the Scripture is plain in so saying. John 1:14: "The Word was made *flesh,* and dwelt among us." Hebrews 2:14: "Forasmuch, then, as the children are partakers of flesh and blood, He also Himself took part of the same." He was flesh and blood as we are, and therefore He is called man. 1 Timothy 2:5: "There is one Mediator between God and man, the Man Christ Jesus."

He was subject to the same infirmities as we are. I do not mean sinful infirmities, but natural infirmities. He was subject to the same temptations, to hunger, thirst, cold, heat, weariness, and sleep. He was true man, not an imaginary or theoretical man, but a real, true man. When the people said, "Behold, a spirit," in Luke 24:37, Christ said, "No, touch Me; handle Me. I have flesh and bones, which is more than any spirit has." And it was necessary that Christ should be true man. I will not trouble you with all the arguments that might be given except these two:

First, it was necessary so that He might have the right of redemption. Man had fallen and needed a redeemer; and had Christ not been a man, He would not have had the right of redemption. Leviticus 25:25: "If thy brother be waxen poor, and hath sold away some of his possession, and if any of his kin come to redeem it, then shall he redeem that which his brother hath sold." Well, we had lost our possession; we lost ourselves, and now, if we have any brother who can come to redeem us, it is his right; but we had none, and were not able to redeem ourselves. We had no friend, no brother who could do it for us. But then Jesus Christ became man, took flesh of our flesh and bone of our bone, and so the right of redemption belonged to Him. And therefore He was man that He might have the right of redemption.

Second, Christ must be true man so that He might be capable of dying for us, of conquering our enemies, of satisfying the law and justice, and of obtaining such mercies as we stood in need of. It was needful that He be man so that He might be capable of death. Hebrews 2:14: "Forasmuch, then, as the children are partakers of flesh and blood, He also Himself likewise took part of the same, that through death He might destroy him that had the power of death, that is, the devil." Had not Christ been true man, He could not have died; and had He not died, He could not have destroyed him who had the power of death, the devil. But, as Hebrews tells us, He was a partaker of flesh and blood so that, through death, He might destroy him who had the power of death, the devil. So Christ must be true man so that He might die, and destroy the devil, who had the power of death.

He must be true man and die so that He might satisfy the law and justice of God. As Genesis told us, "In the day that thou eatest thou shalt die the death." It must be either you yourself, or your surety in your place. One of the same nature as you must die. Since the law was broken by a man, a man must die to satisfy the law and satisfy justice; a man must die to obtain remission of sin. Hebrews 9:22: "Without the shedding of blood there is no remission of sin." Had not Christ been true man, with blood in Him as we have, and that blood shed, there would have been no remission of sins, no purchasing of an inheritance for us. Hebrews 9:12: "Neither by the blood of goats and calves, but by His own blood He entered in once into the holy place, having obtained eternal redemption for us." So it was necessary that Christ should be of the offspring of David, true man, so that He might destroy death, satisfy law and justice, and obtain remission and eternal redemption for us.

Let this comfort us, first, in that Christ, being true man, is sensible of our miseries, of our infirmities, of our weaknesses, and of our temptations. Had He not been man, He would not have known what weakness means, what hunger and thirst mean, what death and temptation mean; but, being true man, the offspring of David, He knew as well as David, or any who were of the seed of David, what infirmities and weakness mean. Hebrews 2:17–18: "Wherefore in all things it behooved Him to be made like unto His brethren, that He might be a merciful and faithful High Priest. For in that He Himself hath suffered, being tempted, He is able to succor them that are tempted." The Lord Christ is sensible of our infirmities. When Saul persecuted the Church of God, He said, "Saul, Saul, why persecutest thou Me?" It is as if He had said, "I am of their flesh, of their blood, and of their nature. And I feel the blows that they receive." This, now, is strong consolation to us, that the Lord Jesus, the Offspring of David, sits in heaven and is sensible of our temptations, of our weaknesses and frailties.

Second, we may with boldness and confidence now go to God, having Christ, who is our nature, standing between God and us. Hebrews 4:15–16: "We have not an high priest which cannot be touched with the feeling of our infirmities, but was in all points tempted like as we are, yet without sin; let us therefore come boldly to the throne of grace, that we may obtain mercy and find grace to help in time of need."

Do you need grace and mercy? Do you need pardon of sin, and grace against corruption? Then you may go with boldness to the throne of grace. Why, Christ is at the throne of grace. Christ who is the Offspring of David, Christ who is of your nature, Christ who is sensible of your wants—He is there. Go and tell the Lord Jesus what temptations you have, what corruptions you have, what guilt you find, what weakness you find in yourself; go and tell the Lord Jesus, and desire Him to commend it to the Father, and He will do it for you.

The third conclusion is this: If Christ is of the race of David, then the Lord Jesus is no mean person, but a very honorable and well-descended person. He is the Offspring of David. David was a prophet. David was a

king of Israel. David was beloved of God, and David was
an eminent person in Israel. Christ is well born and
well-descended. He is of royal blood. Matthew 2:2:
"Where is he that is born King of Israel?" He descended
from kings, from the greatest persons the Scripture
mentions. It was Solomon's honor to be the son of
David; and it is the honor of Christ to be the Son of
David. "Behold, one greater than Solomon is here."
And there are two expressions upon this very account
which help to set out that the Lord Christ is an honorable person indeed:

The first is that He is called "the Branch" in Isaiah,
Jeremiah, and Zechariah. He is the Branch out of this
root, the Branch of David, an eminent and glorious
Branch. Jeremiah 33:15: "In those days, and at that time,
will I cause the Branch of righteousness to grow up
unto David, and he shall execute judgment and righteousness in the land." David is the root, and out of that
root shall come the offspring, Christ, the Branch of
Righteousness, the righteous Branch, or the Branch
who acts and works righteousness, who executes judgment and justice, a Branch who yields the best fruit that
the world ever had. Isaiah 4:2: "In that day shall the
Branch of the Lord be beautiful and glorious, and the
fruit of the earth shall be excellent and comely." This is
the Branch of David, and is called "the Branch of the
Lord." This Branch shall be beautiful and glorious,
beautiful and glorious all the world over; and the fruit
of the earth shall be excellent and comely. Oh, here is a
Branch of Righteousness; here is a Branch out of a
root, the Lord Christ out of the root of Jesse, the root of
David, who shall yield fruit which shall be excellent all
the world over!

The other expression is from Ezekiel 34:29, where He is called "the Plant of renown." This Branch, this Plant, this Offspring of David is "the Plant of renown." There have been many renowned plants in the world: Abraham was a renowned plant in his days, as were Joshua and Moses. The prophets were renowned plants, and several of the kings of Judah were renowned plants also. But Christ is the Plant of renown emphatically. This Plant has done renowned things indeed; this is the Plant who is to be honored above all the plants that ever were in this world. He has done such things as never any did. This is He who took away the sin of the world (John 1:29). This is He who broke down the partition wall between Jew and Gentile, reconciling the two (Ephesians 2:11–14). This is He who laid the foundation of the Christian Church and built it up. Zechariah 6:12: "And speak unto him, saying, 'Behold, thus speaketh the Lord of Hosts, saying, "Behold the man who name is the Branch, and he shall grow up out of this place, and he shall build the temple of the Lord." ' "

It is the Branch, the Plant of renown, the Lord Jesus, the offspring of David, who shall build the Christian Church. This is He who brought in everlasting righteousness. Daniel 9:2: "To bring in everlasting righteousness and to seal up the vision." This is the Plant who yields such fruit as to send the Comforter (John 16:7). This is He who did such works as never any did before Him (John 15:24). So the Lord Christ is no mean person. He is the Offspring of David, the Branch of righteousness, the Plant of renown.

This serves in the first place to take off the offense and prejudice which lie in the hearts of many against

Christ in regard to His lowliness, in regard to His poverty, and in regard to His being accounted the carpenter's son, a fellow and a vulgar person, in that He was reckoned among malefactors and put to an open, shameful death. Many stumble at these things! The Jews stumble; the Turks stumble and say that our Savior was a poor, contemptible man, and the like. But this may take off all prejudice and scandal that arise thence. He was the Son of David, the Branch of renown, He who did such things as never man did. In Matthew 11:6 Christ said, "Blessed is he that is not offended at Me." It is as if He had said, "Why, I am a poor man who does not even have two coats, who has no house to hide my head in, who has no bread to eat; and blessed is he who is not offended at Me, who does not stumble at My lowliness, nor at the scandals and reproaches that are taken at Me. Oh, blessed is he who is not offended at Me, but can look through these and see Me to be the offspring of David, the Plant of renown, the Branch of righteousness, who can see Me to be all in all."

This may serve to strengthen our faith. Many rejected David. 1 Samuel 22:7: "Then Saul said unto his servants that stood about him, 'Hear, now, ye Benjamites, will the son of Jesse give every one of you fields and vineyards?' " He rejected the son of Jesse, that is, David himself. "What does this poor fellow have to give you? He is but the son of Jesse!" In just such a way many reject Jesus, the Son of David, and say, "Why, what has this poor Jesus to give you? He was but the carpenter's son." But this serves to strengthen our faith. We can say with Paul, "I know whom I have believed." We have believed in Him who is the Offspring of David, the Plant of renown, the Branch of righteousness who took away the sin of the world, who sends the Comforter, who can do greater things for us than we can ask or think. We believe in Him who is an honorable person, descended from the best blood that ever was. This is He in whom we believe.

This should serve to raise up our hearts to a higher esteem of the Lord Jesus. Kings' sons are regarded and observed by all the people. The Lord Jesus was a king's son, the Son of David, aye, and the Son of God, too. Therefore we should have high and honorable thoughts of the Lord Jesus. 1 Peter 2:7: "To you that believe He is precious," precious in your thoughts, precious in your desires. A believing soul sees what an honorable person Christ is. Carnal eyes do not see, but spiritual eyes see this Offspring of David. They see what a Plant he is, what a Branch He is. And it should make men and women desirous to come in and close with Christ. Women desire honorable matches, rich matches; and shall not our souls now close with Christ, who is the best match, the Offspring of David, the heir of the world, the heir of heaven? Oh, therefore, let your desires be towards Christ! Close with the Lord Jesus and honor Him in your thoughts; exalt Him in your hearts and lift Him up higher and higher every day, for there is none like Him.

This may serve to let us see what service and subjection is due unto Jesus Christ. He is the Offspring of David. He is the Root of David. He is God and He is true man, and He is the most eminent man in the world; therefore all service and subjection is due unto Him. Psalm 2:12: "Kiss the Son, lest He be angry, and ye perish in the way." Oh, kiss Him and be subject unto Him; kiss Him and obey Him! Manifest your respects unto

Him in every way. Serve Him with your souls, with your bodies. He has the right of redemption. Oh, therefore serve Him.

OBSERVATION 2. If Christ is the Root and Offspring of David, then whatever the Scripture says upon this account and consideration must be made good. There are two Scriptures worthy of your serious and best consideration.

The first is Jeremiah 23:5: " 'Behold, the days come,' saith the Lord, 'that I will raise unto David a righteous Branch, and a King shall reign and prosper, and shall execute justice and judgment in the earth.' " Hear what the Scripture says of the Offspring of David: He shall be a king and shall prosper, and He shall execute justice and judgment in the earth.

The other Scripture is Luke 1:32: "He shall be great, and shall be called the Son of the Highest, and the Lord shall give unto Him the throne of His father David." Whether Christ ever yet had these Scriptures made good unto Him is worth your serious consideration. Was Christ ever yet set upon the throne of David, according to these words? When Christ was here, it was in a state of humiliation. He did not come to be ministered unto, but to minister unto others. He washed His disciples' feet. He was in a state of humiliation. Does it not remain, then, that these Scriptures should be made good? It is true, Christ has a throne in heaven, but that is not David's throne—that is the throne of God. But He shall sit upon His father David's throne. And surely there is something in Revelation 19:11–13: "And I saw heaven opened, and behold a white horse, and he that sat upon him was called 'Faithful and True,' and in righteousness He doth judge and make war. His eyes were as a flame of fire, and on His head were many crowns, and He had a name written that no man knew but Himself. And He was clothed in a vesture dipped in blood, and His name was called 'the Word of God.' "

Who was this but Christ? "And the armies which were in heaven followed Him upon white horses, clothed in fine linen, white and clean, and out of His mouth goeth a sharp sword, that with it He should smite the nations, and He shall rule them with a rod of iron, and He treadeth the winepress of the fierceness and wrath of Almighty God." Whether this is yet fulfilled, take into your serious consideration. This conclusion, that Christ, the Offspring of David, must reign and sit upon the throne of David, serves for two special things—for preparation and for expectation.

1. For preparation: People should prepare and fit themselves for the coming of Christ. Revelation 19:7: "Let us be glad and rejoice, and give honor to Him, for the marriage of the Lamb is come, and His wife hath made herself ready." This was a vision; now it must be made good in reality. Let every soul prepare and make himself ready for the coming of the Lord Jesus. A bride trims and decks herself up, and puts on her ornaments to make herself as lovely and amiable as she possibly can; so should every soul purge away sin and deck himself with the graces of God's Spirit, and walk righteously and holily and unblamably, and so make himself ready for Christ.

2. For expectation: Christ said, "I am the Root and the Offspring of David." And what follows in the next words? "And the Spirit and the Bride saith, 'Come,' and let him that heareth say, 'Come.' " Presently there is an expectation raised. Christ speaks these words to raise

the expectations of all who should live in accordance with this book and expect His coming: "I am the Root of Jesse, the Root of David and the Offspring of David. I have upheld David, and he has had a kingdom. And I am his Son, and I must come. I must sit upon his throne and I must reign."

OBSERVATION 3. The knowledge of Christ under these notions or expressions is of great concern. This is the last declaration that ever the Lord Jesus made of Himself here in the world. And what does He say? "I am the Root, and the Offspring of David." And so He leaves it to the world to consider. It is thus of great concern to consider Christ under these notions. Now, to make it out in two or three particulars:

1. Here are held out to us the two natures of Christ: His Godhead, or His divine nature, and His human nature. His divine nature: "I am the Root of David." His human nature: "the Offspring of David." And withal He shows a great mystery; for, mark, "I am the Root of David and the Offspring of David," and David lies between both. So here, Christ's human nature appears in His being the Offspring, and His divine nature in His being the Root, and Christ the Mediator lies between both; for there must be a concurrence of divine and human natures to enable Christ to be a Mediator. And this is here held out to the world in the last declaration of Jesus Christ: "I am God, and I uphold you. I uphold David and his kingdom. And I am the Offspring of David. I am sensible of anything that is done to My Church and people, and I am Mediator and will mediate with My Father for vengeance on those who shall wrong them, and for assistance for all those He has given unto Me."

2. Herein many Scriptures are fulfilled. "I am the Root and Offspring of David." And so we may see the truth, reality, and certainty of Scripture. John 7:42: "Hath not the Scripture said that Christ cometh of the seed of David, and out of the town of Bethlehem, where David was?" The Scripture has said it, and said it often in those places I have already cited (2 Samuel 7; Psalm 89 and 132:11; Acts 2:30; add to those Matthew 2:5 and Micah 5:2). All these places are fulfilled in these words: "I am the Offspring of David."

Christ bears witness here, to the end of the world, that the Scriptures are fulfilled and made good, that the Scripture is certain and true, and that you may build upon them; for in Him all Scriptures are fulfilled. Therefore, He says, "Let none pull away the Scriptures from you; let none add or diminish, but look to the Scriptures. Build upon them for I am the sum of them and in Me they are accomplished. I am the Offspring of David."

3. The knowledge of Christ under this notion is of great concern in that here you may see in what near relation the Lord Christ stands unto all saints and unto all believers. He is the Offspring of David; then He must be a king. He must be a brother to all the seed of David; for as it was said of Abraham, being the father of Christ, that he was the father of all the faithful, so it is implied of David, being the father of Christ, that he is the father of all the faithful; and David has a numerous seed. Jeremiah 33:22: "As the host of heaven cannot be numbered, neither the sand of the sea measured, so will I multiply the seed of David, My servant." This has reference to what God promised Abraham, that He would multiply his seed as the sand of the sea. David

has a numerous seed. I do not mean his seed in the flesh, but his seed in the spirit. Godly believers are the seed of David, and so they are the kindred of Christ, and Christ is brother to them all.

Will you yet see a clearer passage? Hebrews 2:11–12: "For both He that sanctifieth and they who are sanctified are both of one, for which cause He is not ashamed to call them brethren, saying, 'I will declare thy name unto my brethren; in the midst of the Church will I sing praise unto Thee.' " They are all one, of one God, say some; of one Abraham, say others. And why not of one David? For this Scripture refers to David in the next verse, and both Christ and all who are sanctified are of the seed of David; for he said, "I will declare thy name unto my brethren."

Now in Psalm 22, wherein David was a type of them, verse 22 says, "I will declare Thy name unto my brethren, in the midst of the congregation." So both Christ who sanctifies and those who are sanctified are of one God, of one Abraham, of one David, and of one Christ too. Christ is the brother, and so there is a near relationship between Christ and the seed of David, so that every godly one may say, "Christ is my Brother and God is my Father." This is a strong consolation to the hearts of men and women.

OBSERVATION 4. The Lord honors the memory of the righteous. The righteous and godly are not forgotten of God, but they are in honor with God and Christ. "I am the Offspring of David," He said. Christ makes honorable mention here of David, as He does in Acts 13. There David is brought in with honorable mention, so that you see fulfilled what is written in Psalm 112:6: "The righteous shall be in everlasting remembrance."

David is in everlasting remembrance, and so all righteous persons shall be kept in everlasting remembrance.

Proverbs 10:7: "The memory of the just is blessed, but the name of the wicked shall rot." David's name here was blessed. Christ honors it with these words: "I am the Offspring of David."

The name of the wicked rots. If they are mentioned, it is with disgrace. When you read of Jeroboam, he is called the one "who made Israel to sin." His name stinks. Judas Iscariot is he who betrayed Christ. So as for wicked men, though they may set up their monuments and have their tombs, as they are most forward usually in that way, their names stink, rot, and decay; but the name of the righteous shall be kept in everlasting remembrance.

Christ the Star

"And the bright and morning Star." Revelation 22:16

I come now to these words. Christ tells you here that He is a bright and morning Star. In Scripture He is called a "Light" (John 1:5), a "great Light" (Isaiah 9:2), "the Light of the Gentiles" (Isaiah 42:6), a "Star" (Numbers 24:17), a "Daystar" (2 Peter 1:19), and here a "bright and morning Star."

The Spirit of God delights in this metaphor, in setting out Christ as a Light and as a Star.

Some here, by this "bright and morning Star," understand the divine nature of Christ, His deity, which is bright, glorious, and shining. And so in Hebrews 1:3 that nature is said to be the brightness of His Father's glory; but the Scripture seems rather to point at His human nature than at the divine nature, for it is said in Numbers 24:17 that "a Star shall come forth of Jacob," noting His descent from Jacob the patriarch, and so His human nature. In Matthew 2:2, 9 a star appeared at the incarnation and birth of Christ, which star noted that this was the Star that came out of Jacob. Christ being born, the star insinuated to us that Christ, who was now born, was the Star. But we may take in both His natures, human and divine. And so Christ here does Himself: "I am the Root of David" (as He was God) "and the offspring of David" (as He was man), "and I am the bright and morning Star"—the bright Star as God, the morning Star as man, risen from man.

I shall show you, first, in what respect Christ is said

to be the bright and morning Star, and, second, the resemblances that lie upon that account. I shall then answer an objection and a question, and finally make application.

Christ is compared to a bright and a morning star:

First, because the stars are without darkness. Christ
is never compared to the moon because the moon has
spots. But He is compared to the stars that have no
darkness nor dimness in them. Christ had no darkness,
no sin in Him. 1 John 1:5: "In Him was light, and there
is no darkness." There was no sin in Christ, no possibility of sinning in Christ. In his innocence, Adam had
power to sin, and he did sin. But Christ had a power not
to sin, and He cannot sin. The stars have a power to
fall, but Christ has no power to fall. Christ is without
sin, without guile. The devil himself could not find the
least sin in Him, nothing of his in Him. Now upon this
account Christ is a bright and morning Star, without
darkness and without sin.

Second, the stars sparkle and cast forth their beams.
If you look carefully upon them you may see how they
sparkle and send out their beams, by which they dispel
darkness. So Christ, having hidden in Him all the treasures of wisdom and knowledge, sparkles and sends out
His beams of light whereby He dispels darkness—and
herein He is like the stars. Now Christ sparkles and expels darkness by His doctrine, by His miracles, and by
His conduct.

1. In His doctrine, the Lord Christ had the Spirit
above measure, and was full of wisdom, full of grace,
and full of knowledge. He gives out divine truths,
sparkling truths that are very glorious. He gave out the
gospel. 2 Corinthians 4:4: "Lest the light of the glorious

gospel of Christ . . . ." The gospel is glorious; it is full of light, and it shines. Why, it is the gospel of Christ. And, according to 1 John 2:8, "The darkness is past, and the true Light now shines." Christ is the true Light, and He gave out the true light, the gospel; and He said, "The darkness is past," that is, dispelled and driven away, and the true Light now shines.

Christ is a Star in that He sparkles in His doctrine and dispels darkness. Christ dispels the darkness of ignorance. Matthew 4:16: "The people which sat in darkness saw a great light." When Christ came they then saw the darkness of ignorance; this Star scattered the darkness, and they saw a great light. He scatters the darkness of wickedness, of malice, of corruption and sin in the hearts and lives of men and women. Ephesians 5:11: "And have no fellowship with the unfruitful works of darkness, but rather reprove them." Here is light now brought to scatter the darkness of wickedness and of sin. He scatters the darkness of death. Luke 2:29–30: "Lord, now lettest Thou Thy servant depart in peace according to Thy Word, for mine eyes have seen Thy salvation," said old Simeon. It is as if he had said, "Now I fear no death, nor the darkness of death, for mine eyes have seen Thy salvation." Christ had come, and since He was the salvation and consolation of Israel, the darkness of death was no darkness unto Simeon.

He scatters the darkness of afflictions. We read in 2 Corinthians 4:17: "For our light affliction, which is but for a moment, worketh for us a far more exceeding and eternal weight of glory." While we look not at the things which are seen, but at the things that are not seen—when we look at Christ and the glory of Christ—

afflictions are no afflictions to us. In 2 Corinthians 1:5 we read: "For as the sufferings of Christ abound in us, so our consolation abounds by Christ." Afflictions are not afflictions when this Light comes, where this Star shines. So Christ gives us His doctrine and expels darkness.

Christ's doctrine is a convincing doctrine. John 16:8: "He shall convince men of sin, of righteousness, and of judgment." So in Matthew 22:21 He convinced them and stopped their mouths: "Give unto Caesar the things that are Caesar's, and unto God the things that are God's." And they were all amazed at His doctrine and wisdom.

Christ's light was a distinguishing light. "Verily I say unto you, except a man be born again he cannot enter into the kingdom of heaven" (John 3:3). So in John 8:39, 44: "If Abraham were your father, you would do the works of Abraham . . . but you are of your father the devil, and his works you will do."

Christ's light is distinguishing light in that His doctrine is quickening and converting. John 6:63: "The words that I speak are spirit and life." His doctrine is a comforting doctrine, full of comfort and consolation. Why, this Star sparkles in the gospel, and there is an abundance of glory and light therein; thus Christ is a Star upon that account.

2. Christ is a Star in His miracles. How this Star sparkled there, and filled the world with glory and light! Matthew 4:23–24: "Jesus went about all Galilee teaching in their synagogues, and preaching the gospel of the kingdom, and healing all manner of sickness and all manner of disease among the people; and His fame went throughout all Syria, and they

brought unto Him all sick people." His fame went
throughout all Galilee, Syria, and all the countries
round about. And in Matthew 15:30–31 the woman of
Canaan came to Him and He healed her daughter:
"Great multitudes came unto Him, having with them
those that were lame, blind, dumb, maimed, and many
others, and cast them down at Jesus' feet; and He
healed them, insomuch that the multitude wondered
when they saw the dumb speak, the maimed whole, the
lame walk, and the blind see, and they glorified the
God of Israel." Here is the Lord Christ now sparkling in
His power and miracles, and showing Himself to be the
bright and morning Star, to be God indeed!

3. Christ sparkles in His conduct. Oh, how this
morning Star sparkled there!

He sparkled in His humility. In John 13, Christ
washed His disciples' feet and wiped them. When He
was done, He said, "Go, do as I have done, I who am
your Lord and Master. I have humbled Myself to set you
down, wash your feet, and wipe them with a towel. Here
is an example of humility for you; go and do as I have
done."

He sparkled in His meekness and patience. Oh, how
patient Christ was when they wronged Him and abused
Him in every way! Isaiah 53:7 tells us that "He was dumb
as a sheep before the shearer and opened not His
mouth." And in Matthew 11:29 Christ says, "Learn of
Me, for I am meek and lowly."

He sparkled in His self-denial. When they came to
make Him king, He would be no king. He refused
honor and greatness and glory. When they would have
trumpeted His fame, He forbade them and commanded
them to be silent and say nothing; when they would

have had Him divide the inheritance among the brethren, He would not, but denied Himself. Yes, He denied His own greatness in heaven.

Likewise, He sparkled in His obedience. There He was a sparkling star indeed! There was never such obedience as the obedience of Christ. Philippians 2:8: "He humbled Himself unto the death of the cross." He bore our infirmities. He bore our sins. He bore the wrath of God. He was made an open shame and scorn. Oh, never was there such humility as in Christ. He humbled Himself to obey things contrary to flesh and blood. Who would have obeyed as Christ obeyed? When He had power in His hand and could have commanded twelve legions of angels, yet He obeyed unto death!

So Christ sparkles in His love for mankind. Was there ever such love as Christ showed to the world? God's love is set out with "He so loved the world." Christ has so loved the world as to die for it. Revelation 1:5: "He hath loved us, and washed us in His own blood." Did ever any mother love the child so as to wash it in her own blood? Did ever any prince so love his own people as to wash them in his own blood? But Christ has so loved us as to shed His blood and to wash us in His own blood. He has so loved us as to lay down His life for us, and He thought nothing too dear to part with, nothing too hard to suffer on our account.

Christ likewise sparkled in His pity and compassion towards the people when they came to hear Him. Christ was full of compassion, and would not let them go away hungry lest they should faint by the way. In Luke 19:41, Christ wept over Jerusalem. Christ wept over sinners who would not weep for themselves. Christ sparkled in all these, and in many other passages of His life. And so

you see that He is a Star, indeed, in sparkling and let-
ting out His beams and dispelling darkness.

Third, the morning star is the most eminent star in
all the heavens, a chief star. So Christ is the chief Star,
the Star of the first magnitude. There is not a more glorious star in the heavens than the morning star, and
none more glorious than Christ. In 2 Samuel 21:17,
princes and great ones are called eminent stars, or
lights: "Thou shalt go no more out with us to battle,
that thou quench not the light of Israel." Why, David
was a star of the greatest magnitude in all Israel.
Similarly Senhacherib, or Nebuchadnezzar, or both of
them, are said to be Lucifer, the son of the morning
(Isaiah 14:12), that is, a chief star, and yet a falling star.
But Christ is a Star who is most eminent; there is no
star among the sons of men, no man, no angel who is
equal to Christ. He is above them. He is of a higher
magnitude. Psalm 45:2: "He is fairer than the children
of men." He has more beauty, more glory, more majesty,
and more greatness than any of the children of men.
Revelation 1:5: "He is Prince of the kings of the earth."
Take the kings of the earth who are stars, even great
stars, yet Christ is the Prince of the kings of the earth,
so that upon this account He is a bright and morning
Star. He goes beyond all the stars and all the lights in
the world, and all the lights in heaven.

Fourth, stars have their influences, and let down
their influences here upon the creatures. In Job mention is made of Pleiades, the seven stars, Orion, and the
rest that send down their influences; and the morning
star has its influences as well as other stars. So the Lord
Christ is not lacking in this way, but lets out His influences. Christ is said to have the seven spirits and the

seven stars, and to let out all the graces and virtues of His Spirit. "Of His fullness we have received grace for grace." He sends the Comforter. He is the Head, and has influence into the whole body. This Star lets out virtue into all the inferior bodies that belong to Him. So the Lord Christ is a bright morning Star upon this account.

Last, Christ is a bright and morning Star especially in that the morning star brings notice of good tidings, that the day is at hand. When the morning star is up, then the day is near. So Christ has brought good tidings that the day is at hand and that the night is past. In Luke 2:10–11, at the incarnation of Christ, the angel said, "Fear not, for behold, I bring you good tidings of great joy which shall be to all people, for unto you is born this day in the city of David a Savior, which is Christ the Lord." And what then? Verse 14: "Glory to God in the highest, and on earth peace, good will toward men." The night of God's anger had passed and the day of God's favor was coming. Christ brought back the sun of God's favor and fatherly goodness and love to us. Luke 1:76–79: "Thou shalt go before the face of the Lord to prepare His ways, to give knowledge of salvation to His people by the remission of their sins, through the tender mercy of our God, whereby the dayspring from on high hath visited us, to give light unto them which sit in darkness and in the shadow of death, to guide our feet into the way of peace."

So here good tidings have come. The day is now at hand, and Christ has brought immortality and life again into the world (2 Timothy 1:10), which are now made manifest by the appearing of our Lord and Savior Jesus Christ, who has abolished death and has brought

life and immortality to light through the gospel—and
especially the morning Star in regard to the great day
that is coming, which some call "the day of judgment,"
and others call "the day of restitution of all things."

There is a great day coming. Christ is the bright and
morning Star who foreshadows the great day of which
you hear in Zechariah 14:9: "And the Lord shall be
King over all the earth; in that day there shall be one
Lord, and His name one." This bright and morning
Star is the forerunner of that day; in that day this bright
and morning Star shall be a Sun. And then verses 20–
21: "In that day shall there be upon the bells of the
horses, 'Holiness to the Lord,' and the pots in the
Lord's house shall be like the bowls before the altar.
Yea, every pot in Jerusalem and in Judah shall be
'Holiness to the Lord of Hosts,' and all they that sacrifice shall come and take of them, and seethe therein;
and in that day there shall be no more the Canaanite in
the house of the Lord of Hosts." There is a great day
coming wherein there shall be no more Canaanites in
the house of the Lord. And Malachi 4:1–2: "Behold, the
day cometh that shall burn as an oven . . . but unto you
that fear My name shall the Sun of Righteousness arise,
with healing in His wings." There is a day coming, a
great day, of which this Daystar is the forerunner.
2 Peter 3:12: "Looking for and hastening unto the coming of the day of God, wherein the heavens being on
fire shall be dissolved, and the elements shall melt with
fervent heat." He is a bright and morning Star in the
sense that He goes before the day which shall come.
Thus you see upon what accounts, and in what senses,
Christ resembles a bright and morning star.

OBJECTION. Are not saints and angels stars, and morning stars too? Is it any great matter that Christ is called a "Star" and "a morning Star"? In Genesis 37:9, Joseph in his dream said, "Behold the sun and the moon and the eleven stars made obeisance unto me." Those were his brothers. And in Job 38:7, when the morning stars sang together and all the sons of God shouted for joy, that is interpreted to be the angels who are called "morning stars." So if the saints are stars and the angels morning stars, is it any such matter that Christ is here called a "bright and morning Star"? And it is also said of John that he was "a burning and shining light."

ANSWER. It is granted that saints and angels are stars, and may be morning stars too. Yet this does not at all disadvantage Christ's being a "bright and morning Star." For:

1. The light of these stars is derived from Christ and from God. What the angels and saints have is borrowed. The angels are creatures of God and of Christ. They made the angels, and so they had whatever light is in them from God and Christ. As for the saints, we have Ephesians 5:8: "Ye were darkness, but now are ye light in the Lord." They have their light from the Lord, from Christ and from God—so that this is no disadvantage to Christ. His light is essential to Him; it is no derived light.

2. Their light is diminutive; it is a little light, as from a candle. They understand little compared to what Christ understands. In Him are all the treasures of wisdom and knowledge; in Him is all the fullness of God, which is not true of any of these other stars. The brothers of Joseph had but little light; angels have but little

light. But what is the light of a toy compared to the
light of the sun? Such is the light of these compared to
the light of God and Christ.

3. The light of these is dependent light. If God and
Christ withdraw their influences a little, how dark are
these other lights! The angels stand hearkening to
what God will say to them (Psalm 103:20). They do not
know what to do, and God must give them a word of
command and give them light; and they depend upon
Him for light. So all the saints depend upon God and
Christ for light; and if God does but withdraw His influences, how dark are saints and angels. So you see
that the light of these is in no way derogatory to the
light of Christ. He is a bright and morning Star.

QUESTION. If Christ is a bright and morning Star,
why do so few follow the light of this Star? Why do so
many follow Satan, who is the prince of darkness, and
antichrist, who is darkness himself?

ANSWER. The only answer to this is that men are
darkness themselves, and love darkness. John 3:20:
"Everyone that doeth evil hateth the light, neither
cometh to the light, lest their deeds should be re-
proved." And verse 19: "Men love darkness rather than
light because their deeds are evil." They love darkness.
They hate light and they love darkness. If men hate
light, they care not for the light of Christ, that is, convincing light, reproving light, condemning light. Now
they hate the light and they love the darkness; and if
the devil and antichrist turn themselves into angels of
light sometimes, yet that light is but darkness, and they
love that darkness. They love delusions; they love errors; they love heresies and lies. 2 Thessalonians 2:10–

11 tells us that because men do not receive the truth with the love of it, therefore God sends them delusions, and gives them up to believe the lies of Satan and the lies of antichrist, who pretend to be light, but are lies and darkness. It is no marvel, then, that they follow the beast, Satan, and the world, and run in the contrary way. Thus you have the main point opened.

Application

1. If Christ is a bright and morning Star, then surely it is evil for men not to follow after light, but to go on in sin and works of darkness; and their end will be fearful and dreadful who do so. The very rising and shining of this Star was to dispel darkness, and to show men the way in which they should walk. Titus 2:11–12: "The grace of God that bringeth salvation hath appeared to all men."

This Star has risen and has appeared to the whole world, full of grace. And to what end has it appeared? "To bring salvation, and to teach men to deny ungodliness and worldly lusts, and to live soberly, righteously, and godly in this present world."

Now if men will not see this light, but will live ungodly, unrighteously, unjustly, and wickedly—if men will follow the courses of this world—then they refuse this light. What will be the result of that? 2 Corinthians 4:3: "If our gospel be hidden, it is hidden to them that are lost." If men will not see this light now, when it is so bright, then the gospel is hidden, Christ is hidden, the Star is in a cloud, and the devil has cast a mist before their eyes and minds; they are lost and undone creatures. John 3:19: "This is the condemnation, that light is come into the world." The morning Star is up; the glorious gospel has gone out, but men love darkness rather than light. They love sin; they love antichrist; they love Satan; they love their lusts. And is it not a grievous thing that this Star should shine among us which the Jews do not have, and we are worse than Jews? That we should be worse than heathens with regard to drunkenness, swearing, deceiving, and defrauding one another, and for all manner of wickedness? Oh, this will be the condemnation: it will be easier for Jews and Turks, who do not have the gospel nor own it, than for Christians who have this light, the bright and morning Star shining among them, and do not walk after it.

2. If Christ is a bright and a morning Star, then let us all look unto this Star for light, for direction. It is not good to be in the dark. If you have but a little light in the dark, you account it a great matter. This world is full of darkness, so let us now look to this Star, and the light of this Star.

You who are mariners, when you are at sea, if you can see but a star, especially the North Star, you think it a great privilege and know where you are and how to steer your course; you know from this how to avoid sands and rocks and dangers. Well, this world is a sea of trouble, a sea of sin and of affliction; and will you not look to this North Star? If you will look to this Star, this bright and morning Star, you will sail safely; you will avoid shipwreck; you will avoid losing your souls, which is the greatest loss of all. Oh, look to this Star to direct and guide you over the sea of this world, that you may go safely to the haven of happiness! If you do not sail by this Star, you will never get to heaven.

It is not sailing by your own lusts, your own wills, humors, and fancies, and living as you please, that will get you to heaven. If you will not live according to the light that He has given you, you are undone creatures. So see to it. We are all sailing, either down to hell or up towards heaven. Well, let us take our directions from this bright and morning Star, and we shall never sail the wrong way.

3. If Christ is the bright and morning Star, then He is worthy to be admired and worthy to be magnified, He who is a Star of the highest magnitude, who is the chief Star in heaven. You sometimes stand looking upon a star, or gazing upon the sun and moon, admiring them for their glory, beauty, luster, and the like. Well, here is a Star for you to look upon and admire. The heathens so admired the stars that they worshipped them as gods, and sacrificed to them. Now you are not to do that, but here is a Star for you to admire, to adore, and to sacrifice to, I mean, to offer praises to this bright and morning Star, the Lord Jesus Christ.

The Lord has set Him up so that we should honor Him as we honor the Father, to praise and magnify Him for the Light He has brought, for the great things He has wrought for us. Therefore, mind this Star; admire this Star. He will come to be admired in all His saints hereafter; He should be admired now. Psalm 148:3: "Praise Him, all ye stars of light."

Are you stars? And are you stars of light? Are you godly and gracious? Praise Him, even this Star, all you stars of light. Oh, bless God for Christ; magnify Christ, and lift up the honor and praise of Jesus Christ, for He is worthy above all princes and potentates, above angels. He is the bright and morning Star.

4. Is Christ the morning Star? Then examine whether this Daystar (as Peter calls Him) is risen in your hearts. The stars may be up in the heavens, but is this Star risen in your hearts? To help you discover this, I shall give you a few things by which you may know if this morning Star is risen in your hearts:

(1) You know the light is a pleasant thing (Ecclesiastes 11:7). So if Christ is risen in your hearts, then the light of Christ will be a pleasant thing to your minds and to your souls. The light is a thing that greatly pleases and rejoices. What delight, then, do you have in this Star? What delight do you have in the gospel? Is the gospel, and the light of it, welcome to your hearts, pleasing to your souls, glad tidings to you? The Word of God was to Job and David as meat, and their appointed food; it was as honey and the honeycomb, more valuable than thousands of gold and silver pieces.

And the more bright the light is, the more pleasing and delightful. Dim light does not so much please as a clear light. The shadows, types, and ceremonies of the law had some light in them, but it was a dim light. But now all these shadows and darkness Christ has taken away, and the light now appears clearly. Is this welcome now to your hearts? Can you say, as did David in Psalm 119:140, "Thy Word is very pure; therefore Thy servant loves it"? Can you say, "Oh, Lord, Thy Word is clear light, and there is no darkness in it. Therefore Thy servant loves it"?

Do you love the light? Others hate the light because their deeds are evil; but do you love the light? Is it welcome to you even though it reproves you and condemns

your light? And the more it condemns and reproves, is
it the more acceptable? Oh, this is an argument that
the Daystar is risen in your hearts!

(2) Where this light is risen, there it works a
transformation. All is transformed where this Daystar
rises. Romans 12:2: "And be not conformed to the
world, but be ye transformed by the renewing of your
minds." Why, what light is it that transforms us by the
renewing of our minds? It is not the light of nature that
does it, nor the light of any creature; but it is the light
of life that does it, and there is no light of life but this
light that Christ brings. In John 8:12, Christ says that
He is the Light of the world, and that Light is called
"the Light of life."

It is light that will make you a new creature, and this
begins in the mind. If you are transformed by the renewing of your mind, the mind will be altered, the will
will be altered, the whole man will be altered, and there
will be a universal change wrought in the man.
2 Corinthians 3:18: "But we all with open face, beholding as in a glass the glory of the Lord, are changed into
the same image." We behold in the gospel, that is the
glass. This bright and morning Star arises in the
gospel, and we behold His glory and His light there.
And then what? We are changed into the same image,
even from glory to glory. So it is a transforming light.

You were darkness in yourselves, but now you are
light in the Lord. The Ephesians who were darkness
were changed into light, into the very light of the Lord.
So we too are transformed into the very light of Christ,
so that we become stars and have that very light. As Paul
said, we have the mind of Christ.

(3) Where this bright and morning Star is risen,

there will be love toward all those who have the same light in them, to all those who are in Christ, to all believers, to all the godly, to all who are brethren; there will be love for them all. 1 John 2:8–11: "The darkness is past, and the true light now shineth. He that saith he is in the light and hateth his brother is in darkness even until now." Why, many will say that they are in the light, and that this Daystar has risen in them. But "he that saith he is in the light, and hateth his brother, is in darkness, but he that loveth his brother abideth in the light, and there is none occasion of stumbling in him; but he that hateth his brother is in darkness, and walketh in darkness, and knoweth not whither he goeth, because that darkness hath blinded his eyes."

Is Christ, the Daystar, risen in that man's heart who hates his brother? No, that man is in darkness, and does not know what he does or where he goes. Do you love a godly man? Do you love your brother? Many cannot endure those who have light in them. Their ways are not as our ways; their lives are not as our lives. Oh, then, light will convince; light reproves, and light will reprove the unfruitful works of darkness. Well, if you have light in you, you will love the brethren.

"Aye," you will say, "but who are the brethren? These are hypocrites, and if they had light and Christ were in them we *would* love them."

Well, if you would know who is a brother, turn to Matthew 12:50: "For whosoever shall do the will of My Father which is in heaven, the same is My brother." Whosoever will do the will of God is a brother to Christ, and to all the brethren of Christ. "I go to My Father, and to your Father, and I have called you brethren." That man who endeavors most to do the will of God has light, and that man has life. When men swear, lie, and follow their lusts and the courses of this world, they are darkness and walk in darkness. But that man who walks most conformably to the rule of God's Word is light; he is a brother. But if you do not have love, the Daystar is not risen in your hearts.

(4) Lastly, if this Daystar is risen in you, then you will follow the Lord Christ and the light that He holds out to you; others you will not follow. I say, you will follow Christ, who is Light. Paul said, "Be ye followers of me as I am of Christ" (1 Corinthians 11:1). Christ said, "My sheep know My voice and they follow Me; but they know not the voice of strangers, and will not follow them."

Christ's sheep, those who have light, will follow the light; they will follow the Daystar. When the Israelites were in the wilderness, they had a pillar of fire that went before them in the night, and they followed it. So now, Christ is the pillar of fire. He is the Star that goes before His people, and they will follow that Star. The wise men had a star that went before them and they followed it; and it led them to Christ. But now we must not follow stars, nor follow men, but follow Christ the Star.

Whom do you follow now? Your own wisdom, your own counsel, your own lusts, the examples of men, and the like? Are these your guides and leaders? You are undone, then; you do not have the Daystar risen in your hearts. If it were, you would follow this Guide, who is an infallible light and an infallible guide. Therefore, examine yourselves by this.

5. If Christ is the bright and morning Star, then let us look and wait for the day of which this morning Star is a forerunner. It will be a glorious day, whether it is

the day of judgment, as some think, or the day of restitution of all things, as others think; yet that day will
come, and it will be a remarkable day, a glorious day, a
day of burning, a day of fire, a day to consume the
wicked, a day to advance and raise the godly. And in
2 Thessalonians 2:1 Paul beseeches the people, laying
the weight upon that very thing: "Now we beseech you,
brethren, by the coming of our Lord Jesus Christ, and
by our gathering together unto Him."

Oh, the coming of Christ is a very weighty thing.
When He shall come in the glory of His Father, and of
the angels, to either judge or deliver the world, it will
be a great day, a separating day. Oh, therefore, let us
look for that day and prepare for it. Oh, the saints at
that day will have cause to lift up their heads, for their
redemption draws nigh. Christ said of that day in
Matthew 26:29, "I will not drink henceforth of the fruit
of the vine until the day when I drink it anew with you
in My Father's kingdom."

It will be a day of rejoicing for the saints, but the
wicked shall have a cup of vinegar to drink, or a cup
mingled with wrath. And they must drink it all to their
undoing. Well, seeing that the morning Star has appeared and is risen, and that day will come, oh, let us
look and prepare for it!

6. Lastly, if Christ is the bright and morning Star,
then we should be encouraged here to serve the Lord
Jesus Christ, and not to be weary of His work or His
ways. And though we meet with difficulties and discouragements, we should yet go on and fight it out
upon the ground given us in Revelation 2:26, 28: "He
that overcometh and keepeth My works unto the end,
to him will I give power over the nations, and I will give

him the morning Star."

It is as if Christ had said, "He who goes on in My service, and overcomes the world, the devil, corruption, and sin, I will give him the morning Star. I will make him glorious. I will fill him with joy and comfort. I will give him Myself, for I am the morning Star. He shall have fruition of Me and possession of Me."

So here's encouragement enough for anyone to go on in godliness, in Christianity, in the ways of holiness, and to oppose the enemies of Christ: he shall have Christ Himself, the morning Star.

The Voice of the Spirit and the Bride

"And the Spirit and the Bride say, 'Come.' "
Revelation 22:17

The Lord Christ has declared many things concerning Himself, His enemies, and the state His Church should come to in this book. Here the Spirit and the Bride say, "Is it so? Come, come. Seeing that there are such prophecies of Thyself, come, come; seeing that Thine enemies shalt meet with such things, come; seeing that Thou wilt bring the Church to such a state, come. The Spirit and the Bride say, 'Come.' "

I want to briefly expound the words. Some understand them to be a figure of speech, where two words are used for one: "And the Spirit and the Bride," that is, the Bride by the Spirit, "say, 'Come, come' "; or, the Bride by the instinct of the Spirit says, "Come"; or the spiritual Bride, the Bride sanctified by the Spirit, says, "Come."

But you see that they are put distinctly, and so some expositors render these words thus: "The Spirit says, 'Come,' and the Bride says, 'Come.' " That is, the Spirit who spoke to the churches in the second and third chapters of Revelation says, "Come," and the Bride says, "Come."

By "Bride," both the church triumphant and the church militant may be understood: those who are chosen, called, and faithful (Revelation 17:14), those

56

who had the name of their fathers written on their
forehead (Revelation 14:1), those who had white robes,
and held palms in their hands (Revelation 7:9), those
who made up the New Jerusalem that descended from
heaven (Revelation 21), those who kept the command-
ments of God and who do His will (Revelation 22:14),
those who were the assembly of the firstborn (Hebrews
12:23)—these are the Bride. Now the Church is called a
"bride" because of how it resembles one.

A bride forgets and forsakes her own people and her
father's house. Psalm 45:10: "Forget thine own people,
and thy father's house." That is spoken there to the
bride. So the Church forgets the world and the customs
and fashions of the world—her own people, kindred,
and relations—and forsakes them. Paul wrote in
Ephesians 5:31–32: "For this cause shall a man leave his
father and mother, and shall be joined to his wife. This
is a great mystery, but I speak concerning Christ and
the Church." The Church must leave father and
mother, leave outward relations. "We have forsaken all
and followed Thee," said the disciples.

A bride is betrothed and espoused to a man. She
gives herself up to a man, and so does the Church.
2 Corinthians 11:2: "For I have espoused you to one
husband, that I may present you as a chaste virgin to
Christ." Christ calls the Church His spouse in the Song
of Solomon; she is espoused to Christ.

A bride has her ornaments and jewels about her; she
is trimmed (Isaiah 61:10). So the Church has ornaments and jewels about her; she is trimmed and decked
with the graces of the Spirit, with the righteousness of
Christ. White linen (in Revelation) is said to be the
righteousness of saints. The Church has her orna-

ments, her jewels, and her graces (Song of Solomon 4:9).

Finally, the bride expects to be married, and so the Church looks to be married to Christ. She waits for the day. She is espoused already, and waits to be married to the Lamb (Revelation 19:7). So you see, then, upon what account the Church is called a bride.

DOCTRINE. Both the Spirit of God and the whole Church are desirous of Christ's coming.

The Spirit of God is said in Scripture to intercede for us. And the Spirit of God lusts against the flesh. And here the Spirit desires the coming of Christ: "The Spirit saith, 'Come.' "

The Spirit desires the coming of Christ because, having received from Christ all truth, and having given it out to the apostles, to John, and then the Church, He would gladly have the Church see the accomplishment of what is given out by the Spirit. This will not all be done until the coming of Christ. All truth will not be accomplished, all prophecies or promises will not be fulfilled, till the coming of Christ; and the Spirit, having received of Christ these prophecies and promises, and having given them out, desires the accomplishment of them so that the Church might see it.

The Spirit desires the coming of Christ for the honor of Christ. It is said in 2 Thessalonians 1:10 that Christ shall come to be admired. This shall be the honor of Christ: to be admired by the world. He shall especially be admired by the saints, by those who believe. And the more admirable will Christ be when they shall see all truths fulfilled and made good which He gave out by His Spirit. Isaiah 44:26 says that God is a God who "confirmeth the Word of His servant, and performeth the counsel of His messengers." So Christ will confirm the Word of His Spirit and the Word of His messenger. The Spirit brought it from Christ to John, John gave it to the Church, and when Christ comes He will confirm the Word and make it all good. So Christ shall be honored, the Spirit shall be honored, and the instruments who gave out the Word shall be honored.

The Spirit desires the coming of Christ so that He will be no longer grieved or quenched. 1 Thessalonians 5:19: "Quench not the Spirit." And Ephesians 4:30: "Grieve not the Spirit, whereby ye are sealed unto the day of redemption." The Spirit has sealed men up unto the day, that is, the day of Christ's coming, the day of redemption. Now the Spirit says, "Come, come, that I may be grieved no more. I am grieved in the hearts of saints daily. I am troubled by them. They do many things contrary to My nature, contrary to My holiness."

The Spirit is a tender thing, and easily grieved. The Spirit says, "Come, come." Then, when Christ comes, the Spirit shall be grieved no more. There shall be a reckoning with His enemies.

Here, then, we may see that the coming of Christ is a weighty matter, and worthy of consideration; for the very Spirit of Christ desires it. But so much for that.

The whole Church, even the Church triumphant, desires it. I might insist upon that first.

Revelation 6:9–10: "And when he had opened the fifth seal, I saw under the altar the souls of them that were slain for the Word of God, and for the testimony which they held; and they cried with a loud voice, saying, 'How long, how long, O Lord, holy and true, dost Thou not judge and avenge our blood on them that dwell on the earth?' " Here is part of the Church triumphant crying, "How long, O Lord, before Thou comest?"

Souls have no tongues, but by "crying" here is meant the desires of the soul. They desire that Christ's day might come, and that their enemies might be judged. And they desire that their bodies might be united to their souls and made complete.

QUESTION. Do the souls in heaven, and the Church in heaven, desire that Christ leave heaven and come down to earth? That would seem strange.

ANSWER 1. Yes, the very Church in heaven desires the day of Christ's coming; and what if Christ leaves heaven and comes down to earth? What harm is there in that? For they, being in heaven, see the face of the Father. And, beholding the face of the Father, they have enough happiness there, as do the angels who always behold the face of the Father.

ANSWER 2. When Christ comes they shall come with Him, as you may see in Jude 14: "Behold the Lord cometh with ten thousand of His saints." Here is a limited number put for an unlimited one; that is, the number ten thousand means "with all His saints." So you have it in Zechariah 14:5: "And the Lord my God shall come, and all the saints with Him." Christ shall come, and all the saints shall come with Him when He comes. So it is in 1 Thessalonians 4:14: "For if we believe that Jesus died and rose again, even so them also that sleep in Jesus will God bring with Him." They shall come with Christ when He comes, so that the very Church triumphant is desirous of the coming of Christ.

We now come to that which is more chiefly our aim and scope, that is, the Church here in this world. The Bride here desires the coming of the Lord Jesus Christ.

The Bride says, "Come, come, Lord." You have it so in Revelation 22:20: "He which testifieth these things saith, 'Surely I come quickly.' Amen, even so, come, Lord Jesus."

John desires the coming of Christ on behalf of the Church: "Come, Lord Jesus." And frequently, in Scripture, this is spoken of. Titus 2:13: "Looking for the blessed hope, and the glorious appearing of the great God and our Savior Jesus Christ." The Church looks for, and so desires, the glorious appearing of our Savior Jesus Christ. That which we look for, we desire. 2 Peter 3:12: "Looking for and hastening unto the coming of the day of God." Then 1 Thessalonians 1:10: "And to wait for His Son from heaven." The Church at Thessalonica waited for the coming of Christ from heaven. And Philippians 3:20: "Our conversation is in heaven, from whence also we look for the Savior, the Lord Jesus Christ."

There are many other similar passages. One is Romans 8:23: "And not only they, but ourselves also which have the firstfruits of the Spirit, even we ourselves groan within ourselves, waiting for the adoption, to wit, the redemption of our bodies." We look for the coming of Christ.

Now what kind of desires does the Church has? "The Bride saith, 'Come.' " The Bride desires the coming of Christ.

This desire is a spiritual desire. It is no carnal desire, but is such a desire as is in Christ Himself towards the Church. Song of Solomon 2:10: "My beloved spake, and said unto me, 'Rise up, my love, my fair one, and come away.' " And so it is in verse 13: "Arise, my love, my fair one, and come away."

Christ's desire for the Church is a spiritual desire. Song of Solomon 7:10: "I am my beloved's, and his desire is toward me." Christ's desire is toward His Church, and it is a spiritual desire.

So the Church's desire is the same toward Him. "Come, my beloved, let us go forth into the fields." As Christ calls His Church, so the Church calls Him, "Come, my beloved!" This is a spiritual desire, a desire that the Spirit of God has begotten in her; for the Spirit works gracious and holy desires in the hearts of men and women, and those desires, being put forth now towards Christ, are identified by the Spirit as spiritual desires.

The desire of the Church is an earnest, strong desire. 2 Corinthians 5:2: "For in this we groan, earnestly desiring to be clothed with our house which is from heaven." Paul groaned earnestly while on earth, and in Philippians 1:23 Paul said that he desired to be dissolved and to be with Christ. He desired the coming of Christ to dissolve him so that he might be with Christ. In Romans 8:19 it is called "the earnest expectation of the creature," and verse 23 says that "we groan within ourselves."

It is such a desire as those have who are sick for love. In Song of Solomon 5:8 the Church says, "Tell him that I am sick of love." The Church is sick out of love for Jesus Christ, and earnestly desires His coming. This is such a desire as is in women who are with child, who miscarry if they do not get that for which they desire. Such a desire is in the captive who wants to be delivered; such a desire is in those who are sick and wish for health; such a desire is in women for their husbands who are out to sea. These are earnest desires.

It is a working desire. It is a desire that puts men and women to doing, a desire that makes them work. Here a desire caused the Church to pray, "Come, come, Lord Jesus, come quickly." This is a desire that will make you active; not a sluggish, lazy desire, as is in too many, but a waking desire. 2 Peter 3:12: "Looking for and hastening unto the coming of the day of God." Where there is looking, there will be desire; and where there is desire, there will be acting and hastening to the coming.

It is a desire that is lasting. It is not a humor, a fit, or a fancy, but it is a continual and lasting desire. The Church has had this desire for hundreds of years, yea, thousands of years. 1 Peter 1:13: "Wherefore gird up the loins of your mind, be sober, and hope to the end for the grace that is to be brought unto you at the revelation of Jesus Christ." It will make men and women hope to the end. Where there is a desire for something, there is hope; and it will make them hope to the end when it lasts to the end. The desire lasts until Christ comes.

It is a desire that is well-grounded. It springs from a good foundation; it is not from the fancy of a man, or from a notion, or from a concept or tradition, but it is well-grounded and springs from a good root. It springs from promises; it springs from prayer; it rises from promises. Acts 1:11: "The same Jesus which is taken up from you into heaven shall so come in like manner as ye have seen Him go into heaven."

Well, this Jesus who has gone to heaven shall so come again. Here is a good root, a foundation, a promise now for this desire. Hebrews 10:37: "Yet a little time, and He that shall come will come, and will not tarry." And Revelation 22:12: "Behold, I come quickly, and My reward is with Me."

There are many promises in the Scripture to this purpose. Therefore Peter said in 2 Peter 3:13, "Nevertheless we, according to His promise, look for the new heavens and the new earth." It is a desire that is grounded upon a promise, a divine promise and not a human promise, a promise from heaven and not from earth.

It is grounded upon prayer. In the Lord's Prayer Christ taught us to pray, "Thy kingdom come."

So you see of what nature the desires of the Church are: they are spiritual desires; they are earnest desires; they are working desires; they are desires that are lasting, and they are desires that are well-grounded.

QUESTION. Why does the Church desire the coming of Christ?

ANSWER 1. The Church desires the coming of Christ so that the Lord Christ Himself may be perfected and completed. Christ accounts Himself imperfect in heaven. In Ephesians 1:23 the Church is said to be the fullness of Christ; and until Christ has with Him all whom the Father has given Him, He is not complete. The Church desires that Christ may have His fullness: "Come, Lord, and take all Thine own. Come, Lord, and gather in all Thy saints. Come, Lord, and enjoy all that the Father hath given Thee." It is so that Christ may have His fullness, be perfected, and be complete.

ANSWER 2. The Church desires Christ's coming so that all the enemies of Christ may be brought under, and especially that those grand enemies of Christ's may be brought down, such as antichrist and Satan. They are the grand enemies of Christ. 2 Thessalonians 2:8: "And then shall that wicked one be revealed, whom the Lord shall consume with the spirit of His mouth, and shall destroy with the brightness of His coming." This is spoken of antichrist, that wicked one. When Christ comes there shall be a total destruction of antichrist, and of all who adhere to him. Then shall the prophet and the beast be taken, as we read in Revelation 19:19–20: "I saw the beast, and the kings of the earth, and their armies, gathered together to make war with Him that sat on the horse, and His army. And the beast was taken, and with him the false prophet that wrought miracles before him, with which he deceived them that had received the mark of the beast, and them that worshipped his image."

When Christ comes, the beast and the false prophet will be taken. These two are antichrist. They shall be taken and judged, and that enemy Satan also, as we read in Revelation 20:1–3: "I saw an angel come down from heaven, having the key of the bottomless pit and a great chain in his hand. And he laid hold on the dragon, that old serpent, which is the devil and Satan, and bound him a thousand years, and cast him into the bottomless pit and shut him up, and set a seal upon him that he should not deceive the nations any more, till the thousand years should be fulfilled." Then shall the enemies of Christ be brought under. The Church says, "Come," on that account.

ANSWER 3. The Church says, "Come," and desires His coming, so that it might be freed from all enemies within and without. When Christ comes, this shall be made good. In Revelation 21:2 there was a new Jerusalem coming down from heaven. What then? "Behold, the tabernacle of God is with men, and He will dwell with them, and they shall be His people, and God Himself shall be with them, and be their God; and

God shall wipe away all tears from their eyes, and there shall be no more death, neither sorrow, nor crying, neither shall there be any more pain."

When Christ comes, all enemies shall be taken away—all persecutions, all afflictions, all temptations, yea, all corruptions within. Romans 7:24–25: "Who shall deliver me from this body of death? I thank God through Jesus Christ." When Christ comes, I shall be delivered from this body of death. Thus Christ's coming is desired by the Church so that she may be freed from all enemies without, and so that there might be no sinning nor grieving of the Spirit, so that there might be no tears, no sorrow, no crying, no pain, but freedom from all, both inwardly and outwardly.

ANSWER 4. Lastly, the Church desires the coming of Christ so that she may enjoy all the good things that are to be had by His coming, so that she may have all the choice refreshing that is spoken of in Acts 3:19: "Repent ye, therefore, and be converted, that your sins may be blotted out, when the times of refreshing shall come from the presence of the Lord." Christ shall come, and there will be times of refreshing, times of choice refreshing, such refreshing as our souls have never had.

The Church desires Christ's coming that it may have the glorious liberty mentioned in Romans 8:21: "Because the creature itself also shall be delivered from the bondage of corruption into the glorious liberty of the children of God." Then the children of God shall have liberty, and glorious liberty; never have they had such liberty as they shall then have.

Then they shall likewise be partakers of the great honor that Christ will bestow upon them. Revelation

2:17: "He that overcometh I will give to eat of the hidden manna, and I will give him a white stone, and in the stone a new name written." He shall have a title of honor, as well as a new seat. Revelation 3:21: "To him that overcometh will I grant to sit with Me in My throne, even as I overcame, and am set down with My Father in His throne." Christ will honor the Church, then, set her upon a throne, exalt every member thereof, and give them a new name and a new seat.

They shall have great honor, inasmuch as it is said in Isaiah 62:3: "Thou shalt be as a crown of glory in the hand of the Lord, and a royal diadem in the hand of thy God." They shall be honored as kings and queens: "He hath made us kings and priests unto God." And we shall be honored as kings and priests when Christ comes.

Then they shall have more near conjunction with Christ, and more communion with Him than ever. Revelation 19:7: "Let us be glad and rejoice, and give honor to Him, for the marriage of the Lamb is come." The marriage of the Lamb is come. Then shall be the marriage. Now it is a bride, but then shall be the marriage; then shall we rejoice, for the marriage of the Lamb is come, and His wife "hath made herself ready." There will be more intimate and sweet communion; then will Christ let out His love for the soul indeed. Then He will lead His spouse, His bride, His wife into the marriage chamber, into the wine cellar. Then shall there be apples of comfort and flagons of wine; then the spiced wine will be brought forth. There will be more near conjunction and sweet communion with Christ than ever.

Then shall the Church be made like Christ indeed.

1 John 3:2: "When He shall appear, we shall be like Him." We shall then be transformed into the image of Christ fully. And it is on all these grounds that the Church desires the coming of Christ.

Uses

1. Does the Church desire the coming of Christ? Then this is a reproof to those Christians who do not mind Christ, nor desire Christ, nor look after Christ at all. Many Christians never desire the coming of Christ, but they desire other things. People have their desires carried otherwise. The mariner desires a fit wind to carry him to his port; the husbandman desires that the harvest would come; the lawyer desires that the term would come; the woman desires her husband's return from abroad; and the beggar desires alms. But where is a soul who desires the coming of Christ, who says, "Come, Lord, come quickly!"

It is an argument that you have little or no grace in you; it is an argument that you are no friend to Christ, but rather an enemy to Christ, when you do not mind Christ and His coming, and do not desire His coming. Look at Matthew 24:48–51: "And if that evil servant shall say in his heart, 'My lord delayeth his coming,' and shall begin to smite his fellow servants, and to eat and drink with the drunken, the lord of that servant shall come in a day that he looketh not for him, and in an hour that he is not aware of, and shall cut him asunder, and appoint him his portion with the hypocrites; there shall be weeping and gnashing of teeth." Mark it, this speaks of a wicked servant who defers the coming of Christ, and who does not mind the coming of Christ.

So this is a just reproof to most: they do not mind, and they do not think of, the coming of the Lord Christ. They desire it not.

2. Does the Church desire the coming of Christ? Then this informs us that Christ is desirable, yea, very desirable. The Spirit desires Christ to come; the Church triumphant desires Christ to come; the Church militant in this world desires Christ to come. Christ is very desirable; yea, what is there that is more desirable than Christ? Haggai 2:7 calls Him "the desire of nations." Where there is but one saint in a nation, Christ is desired there. Wherever there are any godly ones, any who are endued with the Spirit of God, they desire Christ. He is the desire of all nations in the world. If those nations have any godly people in them, they desire Christ. Song of Solomon 5:10 says that Christ is "white and ruddy, the chiefest of ten thousand," and altogether lovely. Who should be more desired than Christ?

Christ looks upon His Church as lovely and desirable and says, "Come away, come away, My beloved. Come over the mountains and have communion with Me." And Christ is far more lovely than the Church, far more glorious and beautiful. Christ is the morning Star, and is that not desirable? Christ is the Sun of righteousness who comes with healing in His wings, and is He not desirable? Christ is the brightness of His Father's glory, and is He not desirable? Proverbs 4:7 says that wisdom is to be desired above all things; and is not Christ the Fountain of wisdom? "In Him are hidden all the treasures of wisdom and knowledge" (Colossians 2:3); and is He not desirable? Christ is the Bridegroom; and is He not desirable? He is such a Bridegroom as never was in the world before, nor will be afterwards. It is no marvel, then, that the Church says, "Come, come, come." He is desirable.

3. If the Church desires Christ, then here is matter of comfort for the Church, for every believing soul that desires Christ, upon several considerations:

(1) The soul that so desires Christ as you have heard, that desires Christ spiritually and earnestly, that has a waking desire after Christ, a lasting desire, a desire that springs from promises—this is an argument now unto you of the truth of grace—such desires come from the Spirit of God. They are not from nature, from flesh and blood, for flesh and blood do not desire the coming of Christ. These desires are from a principle of grace, from a fountain within, from something conformable to Christ; and this is an argument of comfort. Many are troubled. They do not know whether or not they have grace. But do you desire the coming of Christ? If you do, that is evidence of grace in your heart.

(2) Desiring Christ's coming argues a blessed condition. Matthew 5:6: "Blessed are those that hunger and thirst after righteousness." They are blessed, in the judgment of the Lord Christ Himself. You are a blessed creature. Do you hunger and thirst after righteousness? To hunger and thirst is to have earnest, strong desires after righteousness; and, if so, you are blessed. Now, is not Christ righteousness? The Lord says in Jeremiah 23:5–6, "Behold, the days come that I will raise unto David a righteous Branch, and a King shall reign and prosper, and shall execute judgment and justice in the earth; in His days Judah shall be saved, and Israel shall dwell safely, and this is the name whereby He shall be called: the Lord our righteousness." Well, do you hunger and thirst now after righteousness, after Christ

and His righteousness? Do you see your own righteousness as being spotted, filthy, and loathsome? Do you throw it away and hunger and thirst after the righteousness of Christ, and what He has purchased and procured by His death, sufferings, and merits for poor sinners? Then you are a blessed creature who satisfies Christ.

(3) You shall be satisfied, for ere long Christ will come. Hebrews 10:37: "Yet a little while, and He that shall come will come, and will not tarry." Revelation 22:12: "Behold, I come quickly, and My reward is with Me." Christ says that He is coming, and He will satisfy the souls of those who desire Him. Revelation 7:15–17: "Therefore are they before the throne of God, and serve Him day and night. They shall hunger no more, neither thirst any more, neither shall the sun light on them, nor any heat, for the Lamb which is in the midst of the throne shall feed them, and shall lead them unto living fountains of waters, and God shall wipe away all tears from their eyes."

They shall be fed and filled; they shall neither hunger nor thirst any more; and these things are not far off. Now it might be objected, "We have desired, and we have waited a long time!" Why, it is not long. Christ is coming. The things that we now see foreshadow as much unto us. "When the Son of Man cometh, shall He find faith on the earth?" Where is any faithfulness in men? There is no faith to be found in men. And does not the devil rage now, and throw out blasphemies, errors and heresies? Are not all nations perplexed at this time, and know not what to do or which way to turn? And is there not a spirit of prayer abroad for the coming of Jesus Christ, more than has been in former days?

And if it is so, these are arguments that Christ's coming is nearer at hand than you are aware of. Therefore, here is comfort to the saints and servants of Christ. Christ will come, and then they shall be satisfied who have desired and waited for His coming.

4. If it is so that the Church desires the coming of Christ, then let me entreat you all to examine yourselves as to whether or not you desire the coming of Christ. And if you would know it, then I shall here commend two or three things to you beyond what I have already laid down:

(1) The soul that desires the coming of Christ, as the Bride in our text does, does not live in any known sin. The soul that lives in any known sin cannot, does not, dares not desire the coming of Christ. I will give you one Scripture for it, and that is 2 Thessalonians 1:8: "When the Lord Jesus shall be revealed from heaven with His mighty angels, in flaming fire taking vengeance on them that know not God, and that obey not the gospel of our Lord Jesus Christ." If a man is ignorant, and knows not God and his duty; and if another man knows God and his duty, and disobeys the gospel, dares that man now desire the coming of Christ, who shall come in flames of fire to render vengeance? Does the murderer desire the coming of the judge? Does any guilty man desire the coming of him who will bring him forth and punish him for his guilt? Therefore, the soul that desires the coming of Christ is a soul that lives in no known sin. He is neither ignorant of God, the gospel, or his duty, nor is he disobedient to God, Christ, or the gospel.

(2) If you desire the coming of Christ in truth, and according to those desires already mentioned, you

will make some preparation for the coming of Christ. When the bride said, "Come," she prepared for His coming. Revelation 19:7: "And his wife hath made herself ready." So it was in Luke 12:40: "Be ye therefore ready also, for the Son of Man cometh at an hour when ye think not." The wise virgins made ready in Matthew 25:10: "And while the foolish virgins went to buy oil, the bridegroom came, and they that were ready went in with him to the marriage, and the door was shut." Now, what do you do towards Christ's coming? Do you purge out your corruptions? Do you mortify your lusts? Do you renounce the world, and the vanities thereof? Do you trim and deck yourselves with all graces? If you do, it is an argument that you desire Christ, and that your desires are right.

(3) Those who desire the coming of Christ in truth and sincerity are glad when there are any appearances of the coming of Christ, any signs or tokens of His coming. Luke 21:25–28: "And there shall be signs in the sun, and in the moon, and in the stars, and upon the earth distress of nations, with perplexity, the sea and the waves roaring, men's hearts failing them for fear, and for looking after those things which are coming on the earth; and then shall they see the Son of Man coming in a cloud with power and divine glory. And when these things begin to come to pass, then look up and lift your heads, for your redemption draweth nigh."

When there is any appearance of Christ's coming, the saints are glad. They lift up their heads and cry, "We shall be freed from all our enemies, both without and within. Now Christ's body shall be complete. Now all the wicked, Satan, and antichrist shall be judged. Now we shall have that refreshment that never was before; now we shall enjoy the glorious liberty that we have waited and looked for; now we shall be freed from sin; now we shall have more intimate communion with Him; now we shall be made like Him." This is that which makes the heart rejoice at the apprehension of His coming. Therefore, examine yourselves as to whether you have such desires of His coming as the Bride has here.

5. The last use of this point is an exhortation to us to desire the coming of Christ, and to say with the Bride, "Come, Lord, come." The Spirit says, "Come." The Bride says, "Come." And if we will not say, "Come," it is either because we are not endued with the Spirit of God or because we are not the Bride of Christ. Besides these points, consider:

(1) It argues love for Christ if we desire His coming. 2 Timothy 4:8: "To all them that love His appearing." If we do not desire His coming, it argues little love for Christ. A woman who does not desire the coming *of* her husband has little love *to* her husband.

(2) The day of His coming will be a marriage day for the soul (Revelation 19:7–9), and Christ will rejoice over His people then as a man rejoices over his bride (Isaiah 62:5). Therefore, seeing that the Spirit of God desires it and the Bride desires it, let us also desire Christ's coming; let us manifest our love for Christ and long for the marriage day.

QUESTION. But some may say, "What shall we do to have such desires begotten in us?"

ANSWER 1. Consider your own sinfulness. Are we not all sinners, full of sin and corruption? When Paul,

in Romans 7, considered that sin was in him, how carnal he was, how he was carried away captive, how the
sin in his members warred against the law of his mind,
and what a wretched creature he was, he longed for
Christ: "Who shall deliver me? I thank God through
Jesus Christ. Christ is coming; ere long He will be here,
and then I shall be delivered."

ANSWER 2. Consider the evils and confusions that
our fellow servants experience. The devil deceives the
nations, antichrist tyrannizes, great ones oppress one
another, much of Babylon is yet in Zion, all her foun-
dations are out of course; and what should the righteous (and all others) do but long for the coming of
Christ to set all in order? The serious consideration of
this would quicken our desires in that way.

ANSWER 3. Consider the great good you shall have
by Christ's coming. It will be a time of refreshing; it
will be a time of liberty, a time of glory, a time of making you like Jesus Christ. It will be a time of the greatest
good to the Church that ever was.

ANSWER 4. Read much in this book of Revelation.
That will beget such desires in you, for there you will
find that antichrist shall go down; then the enemies of
the Lord shall be defeated, and it shall be well with
those who fear the Lord.

I shall now come to the next words: "And let him
that heareth say, 'Come.' "

Of Christ's Coming

"And let him that heareth say, 'Come.' "
Revelation 22:17

Seeing that the Spirit says "Come" and the Bride says "Come," let him who hears what the bride and the Spirit say be of the same mind, and fall in with the Bride and the Spirit, and say, "Come."

The words in the Greek are "the hearing man." Let the hearing man say, "Come." Some refer this to the succeeding ages after the early Church, the posterity that should come after that time: "let all the ages, and all the saints who shall be hereafter be of the same mind with the Bride and the Spirit and say, 'Come, come, Lord Jesus; come quickly.' "

But more properly it takes in all. "Let him that heareth, let the hearing man, let any man who has an ear to these things, say, 'Come.' Let all sorts of men who read this book, and who hear the voice of the Spirit and of the Bride, say, 'Come, come, Lord.' "

QUESTION. Upon what account is it the duty of a wicked man to desire the coming of Christ? Can a wicked man desire the coming of Christ?

ANSWER. Though a wicked man can never cordially desire the coming of Christ, yet it is the duty of every wicked man, of all men in the world, to desire His coming, and that upon these accounts:

1. They are the creatures of God. All men are God's creatures, and, as such, it is their duty to desire God's will to be revealed so as to be fulfilled. Therefore, it is

the duty of all wicked men, taking notice that it is God's revealed will that Christ must come, to desire the fulfilling of God's will, and not their own. Hence it is that they pray often, "Thy kingdom come; Thy will be done," though they do not know what they are praying.

2. They are the servants of God, and have talents committed unto them. Everyone who is the servant of another, and who has something committed to his trust, has the duty to desire the coming of his Lord and Master, the coming of Him to whom he must give an account. There is not a man in this world but has some talent or other given to him. Some interpret the phrase of John's that Christ is "the Light of every man that cometh into the world" to refer to the understanding and reason that every man has. Everyone, therefore, having his understanding and reason from Christ, should desire His coming.

3. It is the duty of all men to desire that God be glorified. Now God will be glorified in the coming of Christ, and it is upon that account that it is the duty of all men to desire it. Isaiah 66:5 says, "Let God be glorified." John 16:2: "They shall cast you out of the synagogues, and kill you for My name's sake, and think they do God good service." Wicked men know it is their duty to glorify God, and they go about it, though they do it the wrong way. But since the coming of Christ is for God's glory, it is the duty of all men to desire it.

But I shall come to the observations which the words themselves will afford:

OBSERVATION 1. The coming of Christ has been made known, and ought to be made known. "Let him that heareth say, 'Come.' " How shall they hear? Unless this is known, and made known, it cannot be heard or desired. There is hardly anything in all the gospel so much made known as is the coming of Christ. Christ Himself frequently spoke of it. John 14:3: "I go away, but I will come again."

"I will see you again," said Christ. John 21:22: "If I will that he tarry till I come, what is that to thee?" It is obvious that He intends to come again. Revelation 2:25: "That which ye have already, hold fast till I come," Christ said to the church of Thyatira.

Christ spoke of His coming, and so the angels have proclaimed and made known the coming of Christ. Acts 1:11: "This same Jesus which is taken up from you into heaven shall so come in like manner as ye have seen Him go into heaven."

Peter proclaimed the coming of Christ in Acts 3:20: "And He shall send Jesus Christ, which before was preached unto you." God shall send Jesus Christ again, and He shall come. Peter vindicated the coming of Christ, which was evidently questioned (2 Peter 3:4: "Where is the promise of His coming?"): "Looking for and hastening unto the coming of the day of God" (verse 12).

Paul is not silent in this business, but spoke frequently of the coming of Christ. 2 Thessalonians 1:10: "When He shall come to be glorified in His saints." Chapter 2:1: "We beseech you, brethren, by the coming of our Lord Jesus Christ." Chapter 2:8: "Whom the Lord shall consume with the spirit of His mouth, and shall destroy with the brightness of His coming." 2 Timothy 4:1: "I charge you therefore before God, and the Lord Jesus Christ, who shall judge the quick and the dead at His appearing." Titus 2:13: "Looking for the blessed hope, and the glorious appearing of the great God and our Savior Jesus Christ." He also speaks of it in Hebrews 9:28 and 10:36–37.

James mentions it in James 5:8: "Be ye also patient, establish your hearts, for the coming of the Lord draweth nigh." Jude 14: "Behold, the Lord cometh with ten thousands of His saints." It is observable that there is not one writer in all the New Testament who does not speak of the coming of the Lord Jesus Christ.

John mentions it six times in our text from Revelation 22. And will you have Matthew, Mark, and Luke give their testimony? Then see Matthew 24:27: "For as the lightning cometh out of the east, and shineth unto the west, so shall also the coming of the Son of Man be." Mark likewise speaks of it in Mark 8:38: "When He cometh in the glory of His Father, with the holy angels." And in Luke 19:13 He calls His ten servants, and gives them ten pounds, saying, "Occupy till I come." So it is very obvious that all the apostles, and all who wrote the epistles, speak of the coming of the Lord Jesus.

Now why is this coming of Christ insisted upon so much, made known so much, and so often repeated?

1. Because we are reluctant to believe it. Men are not easily induced and persuaded to believe the coming of the Lord Jesus. 2 Peter 3:4: "Where is the promise of His coming? Do not all things abide as they did from the beginning?" These could not believe Christ's coming. And it is difficult to persuade and settle men in the idea that the Lord Jesus is coming again.

2. If men are persuaded of this, they are still apt to forget His coming, and to put the evil day far off. Matthew 24:48: "The evil servant says in his heart, 'My Lord delays His coming.' " It is as if he were to say, "He

will not come in my day." So the wise and foolish virgins grew secure: the wise slumbered and the foolish slept, and so they forgot the coming of the Lord Jesus Christ. So we are apt, I say, to forget it and put it off.

3. This is so often mentioned and insisted upon so that we may prepare for it. Matthew 24:44: "Therefore be ye also ready, for in such an hour as ye think not, the Son of Man cometh." The Son of Man comes, and He will come suddenly when men and women do not think of it. Therefore it is to be made known so that people may be ready for the coming of Jesus Christ.

4. Lastly, this is made known and so much insisted upon in the New Testament because it is a ground for patience, and to bear up the spirits of men and women against the cross, against afflictions, against reproaches, against discouragements, and all the hard measures they meet with in the world. Hebrews 10:36–37: "For ye have need of patience, that after ye have done the will of God, ye might receive the promise." They had endured the spoiling of their goods, and great afflictions. So the writer of Hebrews tells them that they need patience. "For yet a little while and He that shall come will come, and will not tarry." Here is the ground of their patience: Christ will come. And so in James 5:7–8: "Be patient, therefore, brethren, unto the coming of the Lord; behold, the husbandman waiteth for the precious fruit of the earth, and hath long patience for it; be ye also patient, establish your hearts, for the coming of the Lord draweth near." This will bear up the heart against all discouragements. These afflictions, reproaches, and temptations will have an end when Christ comes. It is upon these accounts that it is so much spoken of, and is to be made known.

This reproves those who cannot endure hearing of the coming of Christ, who would rather hear of anything than that. Why, is Christ's coming spoken of so by Himself, by all the apostles and evangelists? Does the Spirit say, "Come," and the Bride say, "Come," and shall we not endure hearing of the coming of Christ? It argues an abundance of guilt, an abundance of wickedness and profaneness, an abundance of ignorance in the heart, that it cannot endure hearing of the coming of Christ.

This reproves those, and shows how inexcusable they will be, who, even though the coming of Christ is so made known, yet do not prepare for it. Do you read the gospels? Do you read the epistles? Do you read this book of Revelation, and do you not meet with the coming of Christ everywhere? And what, will you not prepare for it? Christ will say, "What, did you not know that I would come again? Did I not tell you? Did not all my servants tell you of it? Did not Matthew, Mark, Luke, John, Paul, Peter, and angels tell you of My coming? Why, then, did you not prepare for it? You have lamps, but where is your oil? You make profession, and you bear My name; why have you not prepared for My coming?" Men will be inexcusable, like the man who did not have on the wedding garment, and to whom it was said, "Friend, how camest thou in here?" His mouth was stopped. So you will be inexcusable, and your mouths will be stopped, you who do not prepare for the coming of the Lord.

Let us consider that it is our duty to prepare for the coming of Christ. It is made known in the Word, and it is made known to you this day. Oh, prepare for the coming of Christ. Matthew 24:44: "Be ye also ready, for

in such an hour as ye think not, the Son of Man
cometh." Be ready.

What is this preparation we should make for
Christ's coming? There are four things to be done:

1. See that you cast off everything that hinders your
going out to Christ and meeting Him. Hebrews 12:1–2:
"Wherefore, seeing we are compassed about with so
great a cloud of witnesses, let us lay aside every weight,
and the sin that doth so easily beset us, and let us run
with patience the race that is set before us, looking
unto Jesus, the Author and Finisher of our faith." Well,
lay aside every weight, every burden, every sin that so
besets you from going out to meet Christ, from running the race that is set before you; cast off all things
which encumber and burden you, all your lusts and
corruptions, all base thoughts and practices, all sinful
ends and aims that you have; lay aside every burden.

2. See that you adorn and beautify yourselves with all
graces. You know that the Bride in Revelation 19
trimmed herself up and made herself ready; she put on
her best apparel. So you, put on Christ, put on all
graces. When you expect some special friend to come to
your house, you make preparation for him. You will not
only have the house swept, but you will have the win-
dows cleaned and the tables dusted; you will have yourselves washed and perfumed, and be in a decent,
comely posture and habit. The Lord Jesus Christ will
come, and He is coming daily. You must therefore
make ready for Him and prepare your hearts, your consciences, your wills, your affections, and your understanding. The outward man, the body, must all be fitted
for Christ.

3. You should put forth your desires, as in our text

the Bride and the Spirit do: "Oh, come, Lord; come, Lord." The soul that heartily desires the coming of Christ is well prepared for His coming.

4. Lastly, you must wait daily for the coming of Christ. Job waited all His appointed time for the coming of his Redeemer. Luke 12:35–36: "Let your loins be girded about, and your lights burning, and ye yourselves like unto men that wait for their Lord when He will return." This is the preparation that you are to make. Especially see that you have faith in Christ, as Paul said in Philippians 3:8–9, "I labor to win Christ, and to be found in Christ, not having my own righteousness." So you should have faith in Christ and say, "In the Lord Christ I have righteousness and strength. I have none in myself, but all is in Him."

OBSERVATION 2. The coming of Christ is a thing to be hearkened unto. "Let him that heareth say, 'Come.' " Not every man hearkens unto the coming of Christ. Perhaps he hears of it, but he does not hearken unto it. It is one thing to hear it; it is another thing to hearken unto it. To hear is ordinary, but to hearken is rare; and to hearken so as to say, "Come," is even more rare. Revelation 2:7: "Let him that hath an ear hear what the Spirit saith unto the churches." So let everyone who has an ear hearken unto the coming of Christ, attend it, observe, and mind this business, for it is a thing of great concern. And things of concern you will hear and hearken unto; so attend and observe, for the coming of the Lord Christ is of great concern.

QUESTION. Why is Christ's coming of such great concern?

ANSWER. It is of great concern because:

1. There will then be the greatest distinctions made that ever were in the world. The sheep shall be distinguished from the goats; the lambs shall be distinguished from the wolves; and those who fear God shall be distinguished from those who fear Him not. Malachi 3:18: "Then shall ye return, and discern between the righteous and the wicked, between him that serveth God and him that serveth Him not." When Christ shall come there will be a clear discerning; then the difference will be made between the sealed ones and those who are not sealed (Revelation 7). There will be those who have overcome, and have white garments and palms in their hands; and there will be those who have not overcome, and are in their wickedness. Those who are redeemed from the earth will stand with the Lamb upon Mount Zion, and such a discovery will be made of who are right and who are wrong as never was. Then Christ shall say, "Who is on My side?" Then all Christ's friends shall run to Him; and then all His enemies shall hang their heads down.

2. When Christ comes there will be the greatest change and alteration that ever was here in the world. There was a great change when the flood came in Noah's day and drowned the world; there will be as great a change at Christ's coming, yea, a greater change and alteration than that. 2 Peter 3:13: "Nevertheless we, according to His promise, look for new heavens and a new earth, wherein dwelleth righteousness." The heavens and the earth shall be renewed. Revelation 21:1–2: "I saw a new heaven and a new earth, for the first heaven and the first earth were passed away, and there was no more sea; and I saw the holy city, new Jerusalem, coming down from God."

Then shall be the new heavens and the new earth, the new Jerusalem, and there will be a great change and alteration then. The heavens shall have new qualities and new dispositions, and produce new effects. The earth then shall be refined and renewed, and put into its primitive state, and shall be made fit to be a footstool for Christ when He sits on His throne to judge the world.

3. When Christ comes, it will be the greatest distress and trouble to the wicked that ever was, and it will be the greatest comfort and consolation to the godly that ever was. To wicked men, it will be a time of the greatest distress and trouble. 2 Peter 3:10: "But the day of the Lord will come as a thief in the night, in which the heavens shall pass away with a great noise, and the elements shall melt with fervent heat; the earth also, and the works that are therein shall be burned up." What work will there be when all shall be on fire, and Christ shall come in flames of fire? What result will ensue?

You shall see what will happen to the wicked and the ungodly. Revelation 6:14–17: "And the heavens departed as a scroll when it is rolled together, and every mountain and island were moved out of their places, and the kings of the earth, and the great men, and the rich men, and the chief captains, and the mighty men, and every bondman, and every freeman hid themselves in the dens, and in the rocks of the mountains, and said to the mountains and rocks, 'Fall on us, and hide us from the face of Him that sitteth on the throne, and from the wrath of the Lamb, for the great day of His wrath is come, and who shall be able to stand?' "

It will be a dreadful, terrible day for all the wicked ones. When Christ comes, who will be able to stand?

But for the godly, it will be a comfortable day in the new Jerusalem. Revelation 21:3–5: "Behold, the tabernacle of God is with men, and He will dwell with them, and they shall be His people; and God Himself shall be with them, and be their God. And God shall wipe away all tears from their eyes, and there shall be no more death; neither sorrow, nor crying, neither shall there be any more pain, for the former things are passed away. And He who sat upon the throne said, 'Behold, I make all things new.' And He said unto me, 'Write, for these words are faithful and true.' " It will be a day of great comfort for all believers, for all saints, for all who fear God. All tears shall be wiped from their eyes, and there shall be no more death and no more pain.

4. The Lord Jesus Christ shall appear eminently in His greatness and in His glory. Previously, Christ appeared like a servant in a state of humiliation; but when He comes He shall appear eminently, in greatness and glory. Matthew 24:30: "And then shall appear the sign of the Son of Man in heaven, and then shall all the tribes of the earth mourn; and they shall see the Son of Man coming in the clouds of heaven with power and great glory." Christ shall come with power and great glory.

It will be a day of glory indeed, for the world shall be filled with the glory of Christ. Scripture says that "they shall see the sign of the Son of Man in heaven." What is the sign of the Son of Man? Not the cross, as the papists say, nor other fancies of men, but, as you can gather out of verse 27, "For as the lightning cometh out of the east, and shineth even unto the west, so shall also the coming of the Son of Man be."

He shall come with lightning; the brightness of

Christ shall fill the world with the glory of Christ. Christ is glorified, and Christ's coming now shall be so shining and glorious that its luster shall be seen in the world. In Acts 26:13, Paul said that he saw a light "brighter than the sun at noonday." Christ is so glorious, so bright, that when He comes He will fill the world with glory, and that will make it an eminent day indeed, a day of great concern. So, then, you see that this is a day, a time to be hearkened unto. "Let him that heareth say, 'Come.' "

Now what is the use of this point? This serves to reprove those who do not at all listen for the coming of the Lord Christ. Many hearken after anything but the coming of Christ. They hearken for news from all quarters; they hearken after ships from all parts and ports of the world; they hearken after husbands, friends, and relations; they hearken after good bargains, good matches, good houses, good land, good air, and good apparel; they hearken after new fashions and the like. But who hearkens after the coming of the Lord Jesus? This fault is much too common, that we do not hearken after the coming of Christ.

This is also a matter of comfort to those who hearken after Christ, and so hearken as to say, "Come, Lord; come, Lord." It is a matter of comfort to them, for they are of the Bride's mind; they are of the Spirit's mind; they are on the side of the Bride and the Spirit. If someone so hears and hearkens as to say, "Come," then I say that he is on the same side as the Bride and the Spirit.

This is a matter of comfort. Christ will come, and will separate you ere long from all your enemies. He will free you from all your evils. Ere long He shall come, and all tears shall be wiped from your eyes, and there shall be no more sorrow, pain, or death. This is a comfort to those who mourn. As God took care of the mourners in Jerusalem, so those who desire the coming of Christ shall be revealed; they are the sealed ones, the redeemed ones, and they shall stand with the Lamb and be with Him. They shall lift up their heads and rejoice in the coming of Christ while others howl and run to the rocks and the mountains.

Let us all then so hearken to the coming of Christ as to desire it sincerely and heartily. You have heard of it; now hearken after it; inquire daily whether Christ is coming or not; consult with the Word of God; see whether all things are not accomplished or nearly accomplished that are foretold. Christ said, "When you see the fig tree bud, then you say that summer is at hand" (Matthew 24:32).

If an ambassador were to come into the land from some foreign state, how you would hearken! "When is the ambassador coming? What is he coming for?" Well, what if Gabriel should come from heaven? What if it were David, Moses, or Aaron? What if Elijah, Enoch, or Paul should come from heaven? If God should reveal by His Spirit unto you that these men would come from heaven, would you not hearken after their coming? Well, God has revealed by His Spirit that Christ shall come, and come with ten thousands. He shall come with David, Enoch, and Elijah, and the rest of them; and will you not hearken after the coming of Christ? Oh, hearken after His coming and say, "Come, Lord; come quickly!"

You see of what great concern this is. It will be a day of discovery; and it will be a day of distress, a day of change, a day of comfort, a day of glory for Christ. It will be a day of separation, wherein the wicked and godly shall be separated one from another. You shall no more be troubled with the wicked. Revelation 22:15: "For without are dogs, and sorcerers, and whoremongers, and murderers, and idolaters, and whosoever loveth and maketh a lie." They shall be shut out of the new heavens and the new earth. Revelation 21:27: "There shall in no wise enter into it anything that defileth, neither whatsoever worketh abomination, or maketh a lie, but they which are written in the Lamb's book of life." Then there shall be no more a Canaanite, a Jebusite, a Hittite in the land; none to trouble or molest. Therefore, I say, hearken unto the coming of Christ; then shall you see the King in His glory and in His beauty.

But to wind all up, let me tell you that there is another coming of Christ which you will do well to hearken and to desire. Before this personal and glorious coming of Christ, there is another coming of Christ which we are to mind; and that is Christ's spiritual coming, Christ's coming in His ordinances. For Christ comes in every ordinance to us. "Behold, I stand at the door and knock." In every ordinance Christ comes, and He stands at the door and knocks, and would have entrance. "He that heareth you heareth Me." And in the breaking of bread, there is the Lord's body to be discerned. There is communion with Him in His blood in the cup and in His flesh in the bread. Christ is spiritually there.

So in prayer, Christ is there, as He is in all His ordinances. "Now let him that heareth say, 'Come.'" Come, Lord Jesus, and fill up Thine ordinances with Thine own presence. Otherwise ordinances are empty things; they are vessels without wine; they are bags without silver or gold; they are canes without sugar.

If Christ does not fill up His ordinances, they will be nothing to you. Therefore, let him that heareth say, "Come, Lord; come, Lord; afford Thy presence; fill up Thine ordinances. Come, Lord, and bless Thine ordinances. Bless us in the use of Thine ordinances." In Acts 3:25 we are told that the Father sent Christ to bless. So come again, Lord, and do Thy counsel. Christ is wonderful in counseling. He counsels, teaches, and instructs in His ordinances. So come, Lord, and strengthen, for Thou dost strengthen all Thine own. Paul said, "I can do all things through Christ that strengtheneth me." And the Psalmist wrote, "In the way of the Lord is strength." So I say, in the ordinances of the Lord there is strength. In Ephesians 3:16 Paul tells us that we are "strengthened with all might by His Spirit in the inner man." Come, Lord, and comfort.

Christ comforts in His ordinances. He comforts poor, feeble souls, doubting souls, and staggering souls. He comforts them with flagons of wine and apples of comfort.

Aye, let him that heareth say, "Come, Lord, and heal." He heals wounded souls. He heals wounded consciences in His ordinances. Malachi 4:2: "The Sun of righteousness shall arise with healing in His wings." He has healing virtue in His ordinances to heal your souls. Therefore, let him who hears say, "Come, Lord, and fill up; come, Lord, and strengthen; come, Lord, and counsel; come, Lord, and heal." And so you will find the coming of Christ to be desirable to you indeed!

Of Spiritual Thirsting and Thirsters, Part 1

"And let him that is athirst come."
Revelation 22:17

These words are the voice of Christ. The Spirit had said, "Come"; the Bride had said, "Come." "And let him that heareth say, 'Come.' " So Christ also says, "Come" with these words: "Let him that is athirst come."

"You would have me come," said Christ, "and I would have you come. You would have Me come and complete all, and I would have you come to Me who is to complete all."

So the words are an invitation from Christ to those who thirst: "Let him that is athirst come." I shall speak at this time of the thirst.

There is a double thirst: a natural thirst and a spiritual thirst. You are all acquainted with natural thirst; you know what it is to be thirsty: it is the desire for something cool and moist. But a natural thirst is not the thing spoken of here. Rather, this passage speaks of a spiritual thirst, which is, generally speaking, an efficacious desire for Christ and the good to be received by Him.

Now, to explain this thirst, let us consider what is in a natural thirst. First, there is an absence of moisture. As David said, "My moisture is dried up" (Psalm 32:4). Second, there is a sense of it; men and women are sensible that their moisture is spent. Third, there is the knowledge of something suitable to relieve them. And then, fourth, comes actual thirst. Upon these four elements thirst arises.

So it is in spiritual thirst. First, there is an absence of moisture; there is an absence of grace, a lack of what is spiritual, a lack of Christ.

Second, the soul is sensible of it. As Sisera said, "Give me a little water to drink, for I am thirsty" (Judges 4:19). There was moisture gone, and a sense of it, and water to be had, and actual desire. So here, in this spiritual thirst, there is a lack of God's image. We had His image, but that is gone. As Paul said, "In my flesh dwelleth no good thing" (Romans 7:18). There is no spiritual good dwelling in a man or woman.

Third, we must not only be sensible of this, but must also know that there is some relief to be had. What this relief is, Christ proclaims in the gospel and holds out in the Word: the water of life.

And then, fourth, the soul actually comes to desire Christ. When Christ told the woman of Samaria of the water of life, water that she should drink of and thirst no more, then she came to desire it. So a soul that knows Christ to be the water of life, and finds and feels an absence of moisture, actually comes to desire this water of life. Therefore it is that Christ said, "Let him that is athirst come."

To continue, I shall show you why this thirsting is required, show you the nature and properties of it, and then make some application, in which I shall show some differences in how men thirst.

This thirsting is required of men to fit them for Christ, for till we come to thirst we have a fullness of our own, but when men and women become thirsty with a spiritual thirst, then they are empty of what is their own. Until then they have puddle waters of their own to drink, cisterns of their own, and something of their own with which they refresh themselves: their own good natures, their own gifts, their own righteousness and performances. These they are full of.

But when they come to this spiritual thirst they are emptied of all these. There is a breach made between sin and their souls, and so all is let out of this nature. This new wine must not be put in full bottles; the bottles must be empty. When a man thus thirsts after Christ, he now sees that he has nothing to relieve him but Christ; and this man is fit for Christ because he is empty of himself. A vessel that is already full cannot receive wine, milk, water, or any liquor whatsoever; but when a vessel is emptied of all that was in it, then it is capable of receiving something else.

This thirsting is required because men will not come to Christ otherwise. If men are not thirsty, they will not come to Christ. "If any man thirsts, let him come." The full stomach loathes the honeycomb. In Luke 14 many are invited to come to the great supper that Christ had made, the dainties of the gospel, but because they were not thirsty not one of them would come. One said, "I have a yoke of oxen to go and try." Another said, "I have a farm to go and see." And a third said, "I have married a wife and cannot come." Had they been thirsty they would have come to Christ, the Water of Life. But where there is no thirst there will be no coming.

Tell a drunkard who is full of beer, wine, or hot liquids of the best wine, of the most excellent drink there is, and he has no interest in it. He is full and will not come. And therefore, without thirsting, men will not come to Christ. A man who is not sick will not come to a physician, but a man who is sick and full of pain will come.

Thirsting is required because even if men come to Christ, yet they will not drink when they come unless they are thirsty. You may bring a beast to water, but unless he is thirsty he will not drink. So many men may be pressed by arguments to come to Christ, to come to the gospel and the means of grace, but unless they are thirsty they will not drink. When men come to a feast, and there are a variety of wines and drinks there, if they are not thirsty they will fault the wine and speak evil of it, saying, "It is too new, too tart, too flat." They will find something wrong with it. Or they will say that they are not thirsty, whereas if they were thirsty they would drink.

So it is with men and women who come to Christ but are not thirsty: they fault the doctrine of Christ, which is the drink He gives them. Why, you must deny yourselves; you must part with things that are dear to you; you must take up a cross and follow Christ. And their response is, "Oh, this is a drink that is full of lees; this drink has no savor in it, and will not go down easily." Therefore, unless men are thirsty, they will not drink the drink that Christ has prepared for them. This Water of Life is something in which they will see no life. They will reject it and lay it aside. The doctrine of Christ will not go down easily with them. Therefore it is that Christ said, "Let him that is athirst come."

When Christ speaks of reproaches, persecutions, temptations, loss of liberty, and even loss of life for His sake and the sake of the gospel, this will not go down easily with men and women. As Christ is a refreshing drink, so is He a purging drink. The ingredients in the one—the promises and the love of God and Christ—are pleasing things; but the ingredients in the other—afflictions, the sword, death, fire, and things of that nature—are very harsh things, and these are in the purging drink.

Christ said, "Let him that is athirst come," because, though men do come and do drink, yet unless they are thirsty they will not stay with Christ; they will not stay at this Fountain and be content with this drink for long, but will give it over. Many have come and entered upon the profession of the gospel, and have taken upon themselves the livery of Christ, but have not stayed long in Christ's family; they have not liked His diet or His drink, and have gone away again. Men think it a hard thing to be tied to drinking only one kind of drink always, yet those who have the kidney stones will be content to drink such drink as is to their advantage. So it is with those who are truly thirsty after Christ: They will be content to drink such drink as Christ will give them. Therefore, unless men are thirsty, they will not stay with Christ or abide in His family.

Christ said, "Let him that is athirst come," because such have a suitableness in them to what Christ has for them. Christ in Scripture is set out as a Physician, as a Savior, as a Fountain of living water, and is at a throne of grace. Now those who are thirsty have something suitable to this. A thirsty man would have his wounds healed. He who has this thirst has wounds, and I say he would have them healed; and so he will come to Christ, who is a Physician, and He will heal his wounds.

A thirsty man is a lost man, and he would be saved.

Christ is a Savior, and he will come to Him for salvation.

A thirsty man is dry, and Christ is a Fountain; so he will come to Christ for the water of life, to have the heat of sin quenched, and to have the wrath of God which he apprehends to be pacified. And so this man would have the guilt taken out of his conscience.

He would also have his sins pardoned. Christ is at a throne of grace and holds out a golden scepter. This man will come to Christ to have his sins pardoned. And therefore it is that Christ said, "Let him that is athirst come."

Now, let me speak to the nature and property of this thirst.

1. This thirst is an afflictive thirst, a thirst that afflicts and troubles the soul where it is. When men are indeed thirsty, oh, how that thirst afflicts! Men are more afflicted with thirst than with hunger because there is a greater desire for something moist than something dry. Men are more desirous of moisture than of that which is dry; and therefore, where there is a true thirst, there is affliction of spirit. It is said of Samson in Judges 15:18 that he was "sore athirst." He greatly, sorely thirsted; his thirst was a pain to him, a trouble to him, a perplexity to him. So where there is this spiritual thirst, it is very troublesome and afflictive to the soul. Once the guilt of sin stirs, the fire of hell is kindled in the soul; the wrath of God is apprehended; a man sees himself to be lost and undone. This man is thirsty now, and this thirst is very troublesome to him. This is the nature and property of this spiritual thirst: it afflicts and troubles the soul.

2. The nature of this thirst is that it is vehement; it carries the soul with a kind of vehemence after the thing that is thirsted for. It is like the woman who cried, "Give me children or else I die!" There is a vehemence in the desire: it makes the desire very violent and earnest; it is not a sluggish desire, as it is in many people. Balaam desired to die the death of the righteous; the sluggard lusted and did not have. But this is a vehement and earnest desire. Bartimaeus said in Mark 10:47: "Jesus, Thou Son of David, have mercy on me." He was moved with a vehemence of spirit. And when the apostles and some others charged him to hold his peace, he was even more vehement: "Jesus, Thou Son of David, have mercy on me." He cried still louder. So this spiritual thirst in the soul is vehement, and fills the soul with earnestness.

3. This spiritual thirst is full of complaints; it cannot be silent. Jehoram said in 2 Kings 3:9–10: "There was no water for the host, and for the cattle that followed them. And the king of Israel said, 'Alas, that the Lord hath called these three kings together, to deliver them into the hand of Moab.' " And we read in Numbers 20:5: "Wherefore have ye made us come out of Egypt, to bring us into this evil place? It is no place of seed, or of figs, or vines, or of pomegranates, neither is there any water to drink."

We have come into a place where there is no water. So a soul that has this spiritual thirst complains and expresses itself, as in Romans 7. Paul there found sin in himself; he found that he was carnal and sold under sin, led captive, and that a law in his members was warring against the law of his mind: "Oh, wretched man that I am, who shall deliver me?" He was thirsting after deliverance, and complained of his corruption and inquired after deliverance. So a gracious soul in this case is complaining. In Psalm 32:4 David complains that his "moisture was turned into the drought of summer."

"Oh, when," says the soul, "will this drought be taken away, and where is there water to be had? Where is there a remedy?" The soul is full of complaints.

4. Lastly, the nature of this thirst is such that it is never satisfied without the Lord Christ. A true spiritual thirst is insatiable until it has Christ Himself. Christ said to the woman of Samaria in John 4:14, "I have water to give thee, that thou, having once drunk, shall never thirst any more, but it shall spring up as a fountain of living water in thee." Said she, "Lord, evermore give me of that water."

In John 6:68 Peter said, "Thou hast the words of eternal life." And therefore, "To whom should we go?" It is as if he had said, "Oh, Thou art a Fountain, a Fountain of living waters, the words of eternal life. To whom else should we go? We will go to no other; we are satisfied with Thee."

Men who have spiritual thirst will not be satisfied with honors, with pleasures, or with gifts; they will not be satisfied with anything but the Lord Jesus Christ Himself. So, then, you see what this thirst is, why it is required, and what the properties of it are.

Application

USE OF INSTRUCTION. First of all, is this thirst of the nature of which you have heard? Then here we may be informed that there are few spiritual thirsters. Christ

said, "Let him that thirsteth come." If there is a man
who thirsts, let him come. He says the same thing in
John 7:37: "If any man thirst, let him come unto Me and
drink." And in Philippians Paul writes, "All men seek
their own, and no man the things of Christ." There is
no thirsting after Christ. Let me expand and insist on
this point.

There are few spiritual thirsters, for few are afflicted
in spirit, few are sensible of the burden of sin, so as to
be afflicted in spirit. Few have any vehement desires after spiritual things; few complain of the corruption of
their nature; few are restless till they have gotten Christ
and are satisfied with Him. And to make it evident that
there are few, consider these things:

1. A great number of men in the world are worldly
and earthly-minded. These do not thirst after Christ.
No worldly or earthly-minded man is a spiritual thirster
after Christ. Philippians 3:18–19 is clear on the matter:
"For many walk, of whom I have told you often, and
now tell you even weeping, that they are the enemies of
the cross of Christ, whose end is destruction, whose
God is their belly, and whose glory is in their shame,
who mind earthly things." Mark it: those who mind
earthly things are enemies to the cross of Christ, and
do not spiritually thirst after Christ. No, they are enemies to Christ. James 4:4: "Ye adulterers and adulter-
esses, know ye not that the love of the world is enmity
with God? Whosoever therefore will be a friend of the
world is an enemy to God."

If men's love is worldly, and they are earthly-
minded, they do not thirst after Christ; no, they are enemies to God and Christ. 1 John 2:15 tells you: "Love
not the world, neither the things that are in the world;

if any man love the world, the love of the Father is not in him." The love of the Father is not in him; the love of Christ is not in him; he has no thirsting desire after God and Christ.

Speaking of rich men, 1 Timothy 6:9–10 says, "Those that will be rich pierce themselves through with many cares and sorrows, and drown their souls in perdition." Do these thirst after Christ? No earthly-minded man or woman has any spiritual thirst after Christ.

2. None who neglect the means of grace thirst after Christ. And yet do not a multitude neglect the means? They never read the Scriptures; they never hear a sermon (or very seldom); they never pray; and do these thirst after Christ? If they thirsted spiritually after Christ, they would use the means to come to Christ.

If a man was thirsty, he would use the means to get something to quench his thirst. So if men thirsted after Christ, they would read the gospel, study the gospel, and call upon the name of God and Christ. Jeremiah 10:25: "Pour out Thy wrath upon the men that call not upon Thy name." Now when men call not upon the name of God and Christ, and do not use the means, they are the enemies of God and Christ, and wrath is their portion. Therefore you see whole nations that never look after Christ. Multitudes in this town never look after Christ, nor use the means; these do not thirst.

3. Again, no unregenerate man spiritually thirsts after Christ. 1 Corinthians 2:14: "The natural man receiveth not the things of the Spirit of God, for they are foolishness unto him; neither can he know them, because they are spiritually discerned." And if he does not know them, it is the old rule: there is no desire for that.

Now men who do not have the Spirit, as appears in verse 12, cannot thirst. So it is in Jude 19: they are sensual, not having the Spirit. Now what a multitude of men and women there are in the world who do not have the Spirit; they jeer at the Spirit, and others know not whether there is a Spirit of God or not. Oh, multitudes! The greatest part of mankind is on the broad way. These do not spiritually thirst after Christ.

4. Again, those who live and go on in any known way of wickedness do not desire Christ, nor *can* they desire the Lord Jesus Christ. And do not most men and women go on in some way of wickedness or another, making their lusts their god? And they would not have that god destroyed. They say to Christ as the devils did, "Why dost Thou come to torment us before the time?" When men and women walk in any way of wickedness, and it is their ordinary practice, they do not desire the coming of Christ, neither can they. Many things I might instance on this point, but it is too evident that there are few who spiritually thirst after Christ.

QUESTION. But why is it that so few spiritually thirst after Christ?

ANSWER. First, it is because of the ignorance of men and women. The law of God has never entered into their souls; for had the law of God entered to convince them of sin (for by the law comes the knowledge of sin), of the sinfulness of sin that is in them, of the pollution of sin and how it defiles them, of the distance sin has set between them and God, and of the curse hanging over their heads by reason of their sin, they would then begin to inquire and to thirst after Christ. But the law has never entered into them; they are ignorant of the law of God, ignorant of the truths of God.

And where there is blindness and ignorance, there can be no true thirst.

Second, this is because of the conceitedness of men and women. Most men and women are conceited regarding their own goodness; they have good hearts, good natures, and lead honest lives; they are civil and just; they walk unblamably. And these things they rest upon, and so they feed upon these husks. Solomon said, "Every man is first in his own cause." A man is righteous in his own eyes, and a man will judge himself, justify himself, and think himself better than another. We are naturally prone to hypocrisy, to see a mote in another's eye and not a beam in our own.

The church of Laodicea thought herself to be rich, full, and lacking nothing, when she was really poor, miserable, blind, and naked, lacking all things. It is natural for men and women to think well of themselves. The Pharisee fasts twice a week, and is not like the publican. It is typical of us all to think too well of ourselves. And hence it is that men and women do not thirst after Christ, but will be their own saviors and so undo themselves.

Third, this is because of men's and women's mistakes about God and the creature.

Regarding God, they think God is like themselves. Psalm 50:21: "Thou thoughtest that I was such a one as thyself, but I will reprove thee, and set thy sins in order before thee, and I will tear thee in pieces, and none shall deliver thee unless thou do otherwise than so." We think that God is all mercy, and that he is not so holy, so just, so severe and rigid against sin. Oh, it is but a saying: "Lord, have mercy upon us, and all will do well." Now there is their mistake about God, for God is exceedingly holy and He is wonderfully severe. God's thoughts are not as our thoughts. A man judges well of himself, but God will send him to hell for judging well of himself. The wrath of God is revealed from heaven against all unrighteousness, even the very appearances of evil. God has cut men off for small sins.

Regarding the creature, people do not see the utter insufficiency in all creatures to relieve them, and therefore they depend upon creatures. One man trusts in his estate and riches; the rich man's wealth is his strong tower. Another man rests in his wisdom and policy; another trusts his strength; another trusts his alms and good works; and yet another thinks he shall never die—he is not so old but he may live another month or year. Men are not convinced of the insufficiency of all things to relieve and deliver them but the Lord Jesus Christ. If they were satisfied that no angel, no potentate, no action of their own or action of others, not all the saints in the world can deliver one soul, then they would hunger and thirst after Christ; but while they are not convinced of the insufficiency of all these things, there is no thirsting after Christ.

Fourth, this is because they do not understand the infinite worth, excellency, and good that are to be found in the Lord Jesus Christ alone. They think that they must join something to Christ: "I will do a little, and Christ shall do the rest." They set themselves up with Christ and make themselves equal to Christ. They must save themselves in part, and Christ must save them in part. But if men and women understood the excellency of Christ, the fullness of Christ, the grace of Christ, the mercy and love of Christ, and the virtue of Christ—how the only way to gain pardon, peace, life, strength, comfort, and whatsoever their souls stand in need of is in Christ—then they would be carried after Christ.

Is He not held out in the gospel to be a Sun, having all light in Him? Is He not held out to have life in Himself, all spiritual life in Him? "I am come that ye might have life, and have it more abundantly." Is not Christ held out to be the great High Priest who offered Himself as a sacrifice, and such a sacrifice that all other sacrifices have ceased? All lies upon Christ; and whatsoever your sins are, whatsoever your nakedness and poverty are, there is relief to be had in Christ. He is righteousness; He is strength; He is bread; He is all. So the problem is that people do not understand well the worth of Christ, and all that is to be had in Him. For the Lord has sealed Him, sent Him, set Him forth, and declared, "There is no name given under heaven by which you can have salvation but Christ." It is not in the Spirit of God, but in Christ who sends the Spirit. The very Spirit comes from Christ, so that all salvation is in Him.

Fifth, and last, people do not hunger and thirst after Christ spiritually because they look upon the doctrine and discipline of Christ as unsuitable to them. Christ's doctrine is a hard doctrine, a severe doctrine. Christ's discipline and government they will not endure; they will not endure to bear His yoke. "What? A yoke to come upon our necks? That is intolerable! What? Must I give myself up to Christ and follow Him? Farewell to all comforts, all pleasures, and all delights."

Now because Christ's discipline and doctrine is cross to flesh and blood, therefore they do not spiritually desire Christ. So, then, there are but few spiritual thirsters; and you see why there are so few.

USE OF EXAMINATION. We must examine ourselves as to whether we are spiritual thirsters or not, so that we may have this sweet invitation from Christ, "Let him that is athirst come." Christ will say to your soul, "Come, come." So I say, let us examine and make inquiry whether we are spiritual thirsters or not.

But before I come to the discovery of it, let me tell you that there is both a false thirst and a true thirst. The true thirst arises from the sense and feeling of want of moisture throughout the whole man. This one is natural; the other is accidental. Accidental thirst is when a man's stomach has some type of illness in it, and his palate is thrown off. Then there arises a false thirst, because the illness causes a feeling of drought there.

So it is in a man's spiritual thirsting. A true thirsting arises from a desire for union with the Lord Jesus Christ through a general sense of sin. The false thirst arises either from apprehensions of wrath, of guilt, of condemnation, and punishment—and so causes the conscience to ache, and thereupon that man desires Christ—or else from the good in the gospel propounded, which tickles his fancy, which is, as it were, the palate or throat of the soul, and thereupon he desires Christ. So that there is a false spiritual thirst (as you may call it) in some sense as well as a true spiritual thirst.

1. If you would know whether you are true spiritual thirsters, inquire whether your thirsts arise from the whole man. In true thirst, though the stomach or the appetite is what seems to be craving, that is because it is the first receptacle; not only is the stomach dry, but ev-

ery member of your body is dry, and the whole body must be replenished. In the soul, when the thirst is truly spiritual, it is a thirst of the whole soul—not a thirst of any one faculty, or of the affections or conscience or will alone, but the whole soul thirsts after Christ. "My soul thirsteth after God," said David.

In another person it is a partial thirst. Perhaps his conscience aches, and he thirsts for Christ to relieve his conscience, and if his guilt is taken away he is well. Or, it may be, he is thirsty in his understanding; he thirsts for more light because he sees some error in some way. Or he would have more abilities and gifts, and so it is a partial thirst. But if it is a true spiritual thirst, it is a thirst of the whole soul. The conscience thirsts and would have the blood of Christ to sprinkle it; the understanding thirsts, and would have the knowledge of Christ completed in it. It is a total thirst.

2. You may distinguish the true spiritual thirst from the false one by the rise of the thirst. Both these thirsts may arise from the same cause, yet have a differing way. True thirst arises from sin, and so does the other. But in him who truly thirsts after Christ, the thirst rises first from the pollution of sin, from the separation sin makes, and from the offense sin gives.

It arises from the pollution of sin. That person who has a true spiritual thirst sees that sin has so defiled the soul, so defiled the whole man, that he is unfit for God, unfit for all that is spiritual. And now, because he is so defiled, so blackened and smeared with the blackness of sin, his soul thirsts after the blood of Christ, after the Spirit of God and Christ. His thirst arises from the consideration of the pollution of sin.

His thirst arises from the consideration of the separation sin has made: "This sin has made a breach between God and my soul, and has separated me from God, who is the infinite good, the only good. Oh, it has put me at a great distance from God, and therefore my soul thirsts to have communion with God again."

And this thirst rises from the offense of sin. Oh, it has caused God to frown and be angry. His thirst rises from these considerations, and therefore he thirsts after Christ. But another man's thirst rises from the consequences of sin: "Oh, sin will damn me; it will bring plagues and judgments; sin will make me lie roaring in hell forever; sin brings shame upon me," and the like. So this man thirsts after Christ upon this account: "I desire Christ so that the punishment may be taken away, that I may be kept out of hell, and that I may not be ashamed." So this thirst arises from sin also, but upon different grounds and considerations.

We may also distinguish between these thirsts by the consideration of what is thirsted after as well as from what the thirst arises. Where the true thirst is, it thirsts after grace, after holiness, after communion with God, after the excellencies of God and Christ. Mark it, where the false thirst is, it is seeking purely after pardon, after peace, and after comfort. This is a false thirst.

But where the thirst is true, it thirsts after holiness, grace, communion with God, and the excellencies of God—to be healed as well as saved. David said, "Heal my soul, for I have sinned against Thee." He was saying, "My soul is thirsty, Lord; heal my soul." It is not pardon that heals the soul, nor peace that heals the soul, but it is grace and holiness that heal the soul; it is grace and holiness that make you like God, that make you such as you should be.

Another man does not care for holiness or grace. He would have pardon, ease, peace, and salvation; but as for holiness, grace, and communion with God, these things are laid aside. So here is the difference between them: the true thirst carries you to grace, holiness, and communion with God; it makes you look at the excellencies of God, whereas the other makes you look for peace, ease, salvation, and the like.

Now it is true that men and women who look at grace, holiness, and communion with God shall have pardon, peace, and salvation, but these are as consequences. "Lord," says the soul, "make me holy rather than pardon me; for if I am not holy, what shall I do in heaven? If I am holy, I cannot miscarry in hell." A holy soul shall never feel pain though it is in hell, and a corrupt soul shall never find joy though it is in heaven. In this, then, there lies a great difference.

Of Spiritual Thirsting and Thirsters, Part 2

"Let him that is athirst come."
Revelation 22:17

We now proceed to show you how you shall know the true spiritual thirst by the effects and fruits of it.

1. True spiritual thirst causes fainting in the soul, as natural thirst makes a man or woman faint. It is said in Judges 15:19 that Samson drank and was revived; his spirit came again. His spirit was gone and he was ready to faint; his thirst was such that it brought him low. Psalm 107:5: "Hungry and thirsty, their souls fainted in them." These people were very feeble; they were brought low with hunger and thirst. And where there is this thirst, the soul is brought low; it is ready to faint. So it was with the spouse in Solomon's Song: "Tell him that I am sick of love." It is as if she had said, "Oh, my desires are such after Christ, my Beloved, that I am sick of love. I am ready to faint."

In Psalm 42, David's soul panted and thirsted after God as the deer, when it is hunted, is wearied and dry and pants after the water brooks. So a soul who has a spiritual thirst is ready to faint with longing after God, with longing after Christ, with desires after grace, with the coming of His Spirit, after the light of His countenance, and after communion with God in Christ. This is one effect of it.

2. This thirst will cause men to stir, and to seek out

that which will pacify it. When men are truly and thoroughly thirsty, they will seek out drink. A man who is thoroughly thirsty will get out of his bed at midnight and go down to the cellar and get something to drink to quench his thirst. When men are thirsty they will run to this brook and to that brook for water. Those in Judges 7 were down on their knees lapping up water.

What shifts men at sea will make to get a little water when they are dry! So the soul that is thirsty will not sit still, but will seek out drink. It will seek for brooks and fountains; it will run to every ordinance, to every promise; it will run to Christ and look up to God. If there is any means of grace in a land, it will find it out; if the vision is never so rare, the Word never so precious, it will look after it. A soul that is thirsty will seek abroad; it will not be restrained and kept within bounds. That is the nature of a spiritual thirst. When their desires were a little stirred at Christ's coming, how the people flocked after Christ and stayed with Him for days! Christ said, "You have been with Me these two or three days." And He worked a miracle to satisfy them so that they might not faint on their way home. The people sat with Paul all night when he preached the gospel so that they might drink large draughts of that heavenly doctrine. A soul that is thirsty will seek out relief.

3. Where there is true thirst, men will part with anything to relieve it. Hungry and thirsty men will part with anything for those necessities required by nature. When Hagar saw the bottle empty and her child ready to perish, she cast the child under one of the shrubs, and went and sat down against him. She said, "Let me not see the death of the child," lifting up her voice and

weeping. What would Hagar have given for a bottle of water, for a morsel of bread? And when her eyes saw the well, how it made her rejoice!

When Esau was hungry and thirsty, he gave away his birthright. He sold it for a little pottage and some drink. He would give anything for relief and help in his case. So in this spiritual thirst, men will part with anything to have that thirst satisfied. They will accept Christ on His own terms; they will pluck out a right eye, cut off a right hand or foot, and part with their dearest lusts to have the thirst of their souls quenched.

The young man who came to Christ asked, "Good Master, what shall I do to inherit eternal life?" It was a false thirst in him, as was evidenced when Christ said to him, "Go and sell all that thou hast, and give to the poor, and thou shalt have treasure in heaven." Had his thirst been true, he would have parted with his riches for Christ. The disciples parted with all. They said, "Master, we have parted with all and followed Thee." The soul that is truly thirsty will let all go to have its thirst satisfied. "How can ye believe," said Christ, "when ye seek honor one of another?" Let go of your honor; let go of your pleasures; let go of the creatures; seek honor from God alone. If men were thirsting after divine enjoyments and honors, they would let these things go. Spiritual thirst will cause men to part with anything.

4. Those who are truly thirsty find that things that are bitter to others seem pleasant to them. Drink which is sour and distasteful to others is wonderfully sweet and pleasing to them. When Darius and his nobles were dry, they drank puddle water and thought that no wine was as pleasant as that water. Unpleasant things

will be delightful to such souls. And where this spiritual thirst is, there is no truth in all the gospel—though it seems never so severe, never so cross to nature, never so contrary to our wills, humours, and fancies—but we will drink it down. "Let a man deny himself, take up his cross, and follow Christ"—this will go down with a man who is truly thirsty. "A man becomes a fool that he may become wise"—this will go down with a man who is truly thirsty.

The gospel has many things in it which, to flesh and blood, are somewhat hard and unsavory; but were we truly spiritual thirsters, thirsting after Christ, we would drink even the most bitter truths and the tartest cup that Christ presents to the sons of men would be drunk by them. "To the hungry soul, every bitter thing is sweet" (Proverbs 27:7). So, to the thirsty soul, every bitter thing is sweet. For a man to love his enemies, to bless those who curse him, to pray for those who persecute him, to do good to those who hate him—these things are very hard for flesh and blood. But a soul that is thirsty for Christ drinks down these truths and finds sweetness in them.

5. This spiritual thirst extinguishes in a great measure (if not wholly) thirst after other things; it extinguishes all sinful thirsts, and corrects and moderates all other thirsts. The light and heat of the sun put out the light and heat of the fire, and abate it in a great measure when the sun shines upon it. So where this thirst comes for spiritual things, and is in truth, it abates and extinguishes the thirst after unlawful things, and very much abates desires after other things. Christ said to the woman at the well in John 4:14, "Whosoever drinketh of the water that I shall give him

shall never thirst." He shall never thirst as he had before, shall never have such strong desires after other
things. In Philippians 3:8 Paul said of the things which
before seemed good and excellent, and were great privi-
leges and prerogatives to him, "I account all loss and
dung now for the excellency of the knowledge of Christ
Jesus." It is as if he had said, "I have another thirst begotten in me now, and this thirst has abated my thirst
for the world, for desires after creaturely things, and for
any delights in them. I have a thirst that carries me after higher and more excellent things than they are."
We can see why in Galatians 6:14 he said, "God forbid
that I should glory save in the cross of our Lord Jesus
Christ, by whom the world is crucified unto me, and I
unto the world."

Paul said, "I thirst no more after the world. It is crucified to me, and I am crucified to it. It is Christ I thirst
after, to know the power of His death and resurrection,
to know Christ more." This abated and cooled his desire and affections towards all external things, and the
glory of the world.

6. Where this spiritual thirst is, the more you drink
the more it is increased; and this seems strange. Where
this thirst is present, other thirsts are abated, but this
one increases. The more you drink, still the more you
thirst. The more grace any man retains, the more eager
he is after grace still; the more thirsty after Christ this
day, the more thirsty after Christ the next. This thirst
begets thirst; it makes a man see his need of Christ, and
of grace, God, and spiritual things more and more; it
enlarges his desire. When you throw water upon lime, it
makes the lime burn more. So when the soul thirsts,
and God gives it the water of life, it thirsts more; and

therefore God says, "Open your mouth wide and I will fill it" (Psalm 81:10).

God will fill it in time, but grace stretches our desires and makes men more vigorous in pursuit of heavenly things than ever before. That man or woman who can sit down content with a little knowledge, with a little measure of grace, with a little degree of faith, with a little portion of the Spirit—that man in truth has none of those things, for it is the nature of grace to make one more hungry, more thirsty, more desirous. It will draw the soul out more strongly after Christ. The spouse is never so affected with Christ as after she has tasted the love of Christ.

7. Where this thirst is in truth, it breeds in the soul a conformity to the thirst that is in God and in Christ.

QUESTION. Are God and Christ thirsty?

ANSWER. Yes, God Himself is thirsty and Christ is thirsty. Psalm 81:13: "Oh, that My people had hearkened unto Me, and Israel had walked in My ways." Here is God's thirst: "Oh, that there were such a heart in this people." Where there is a true spiritual thirst, there is a conformity in the heart unto God. In Psalm 119:5, David, who had this thirst, said, "Oh, that my ways were directed to keep Thy statutes." It is as if he had said, "Lord, this is Thy desire, that men should keep Thy statutes. And, Lord, here is my desire. Oh, that I could keep Thy statutes."

Here is a conformity between God and the soul that is thirsty. God says in Psalm 27:8, "Seek ye My face." And David's heart answered, "Thy face, Lord, will I seek." Here is a conformity between God's desire and man's desire.

In the Song of Solomon, the spouse said, "My

beloved is mine, and his desire is toward me" (7:10). And in another place, "I am my beloved's, and my beloved is mine" (6:3). Does Christ desire me? Why, I desire Christ, said the spouse. So this spiritual thirst breeds a conformity between the heart and God: what God desires, it desires.

8. This spiritual thirst causes men to thirst after God for Himself, and Christ for Himself. Many thirst after God, not for Himself, but for themselves. They thirst after the loaves; they thirst after the gifts of God. Many seek to be in great services, or to be in great men's houses and courts, and that they may have their livery, that they may eat and drink of the best, that they may live at ease, but not because they love the person. Shimei came to David and Solomon not out of love to them, but to save his own life. Similarly, many come to God so that they may be saved from hell and damnation; but they would live in their lusts, have their wills, have their ease, and bear God's livery. They have some outward profession, but they come to God not for love of Him, for love of holiness, for love of truth, or for love of Jesus Christ. But the soul that is truly thirsty must have God Himself and for Himself. He knows that all other things will come in afterwards. He says, "If I have God, I have all; if I have not God, I have nothing that will do me good."

9. Last, where this true spiritual thirst is present, it wishes that a man may be satisfied, and that a man may be fruitful like the earth. Why is the earth dry, thirsting after the rain, gaping sometimes as if it would swallow up the very heavens? It is so that it may be satisfied with the rain and be very fruitful. So a soul that has this spiritual thirst desires to receive from God so that it may be

fruitful. Oh, it cannot bring forth good fruit, and that is a burden to it; it longs to be fruitful, and thirsts to receive some influences of grace, some dew from heaven, so that, being watered and moistened, it may grow and yield good fruit. And thus you see some effects and fruits of this spiritual thirst, and so know the truth as to whether you have this thirst or not.

QUESTION. I do not find this thirst in my soul. What shall I think of myself? Others may have strong thirstings, and desires such as you speak of, but as for me I do not find them.

ANSWER. There is a difference in men with regard to this spiritual thirst, just as there is with regard to natural thirst. Some bodies are more thirsty than others. Choleric bodies are more thirsty than phlegmatics, and some Christians are more thirsty than others. Some have lived very profane lives, in scandalous courses, and have run into exorbitant ways. Some have greatly dishonored God, and if God ever stirs in their hearts and brings them to thirst, their thirst will be vehement; it will be afflictive; their thirst will be stronger than other men's.

Some are trained up from the cradle in the ways of God. They have more ingenuous natures, and do not break out into such ill ways. Their thirst is more moderate and less discernible. It is not the degree of the thirst, but the truth of the thirst that is required. Though you do not have a strong thirst, yet you have a true thirst. It is not a strong faith, but a true faith that is required for salvation. Now the degree of thirst which will bring you to Christ, which will make you come and drink and stay with Christ, that is the sufficient degree.

USE OF EXHORTATION. Men and women, oh, labor to be true thirsters after Christ. We can thirst after other things: one thirsts after this, another after that, and another after another thing; all the things in the world are thirsted after by one or another. But who thirsts after Christ? All seek their own, and none seek the things of Christ. They neither thirst after Christ nor anything that belongs to Christ.

At this point I shall endeavor to do several things: give you grounds why you should thirst after Christ, give some directions to those who never thirsted, and give some directions to those who do thirst so that they may thirst more.

As for the grounds, blessedness is attached to thirsting. Would you not be blessed, all of you? Would you not have a blessing from the mouth of our dear Savior? Matthew 5:6: "Blessed are those that hunger and thirst after righteousness." It may be that you do not have righteousness yet, but do you hunger and thirst for it? Truth itself, the Lord Jesus, says, "Blessed is the man, blessed is the woman, who hungers and thirsts for righteousness." And is there nothing in a blessing pronounced by Him? The word "blessed" is a comprehensive word; all good is wrapped up in it—all good for the body, all good for the soul, all good for the present, and all good for the future. If you would therefore have such a blessedness as this, oh, hunger and thirst after Christ and His excellencies!

Also, many great and precious promises are made to thirsters, and will be made good to thirsters. Isaiah 44:3–4: "I will pour water upon him that is athirst, and floods upon the dry ground. I will pour My Spirit upon thy seed and My blessing upon thine offspring, and they shall spring up as among the grass, as willows by the watercourses." He is saying, "I will pour water upon him who is thirsty," that is, "I will pour My Spirit upon him" (that is what is meant by the water here). If you are thirsty, God will not only give His Spirit, but pour out His Spirit. The phrase denotes an abundance; it notes vehemence, such a measure of the Spirit as shall overcome your corruptions and your sins. God will pour His Spirit upon you. So we read in Isaiah 41:17–18: "When the poor and the needy seek water, and there be none, and their tongue faileth for thirst, I the Lord will hear them. I the God of Israel will not forsake them. I will open rivers in high places."

If you are thirsty, if you are even fainting, if you are brought low in your longings and desires after grace and holiness and the things of heaven, the Lord is saying to you, "I will hear you. My ear shall be open. My hand shall be stretched out. I will not forsake you. I will not leave you in that condition. I will relieve you." Sweet and choice promises are made to souls that hunger and thirst; they shall be satisfied.

We should labor for this thirst because the invitation here is to thirsters. "If any man thirst, let him come." And John 7:37: "If any man thirst, let him come unto Me and drink." The Lord invites such persons. When He made a great feast in Luke 14, He invited all sorts, but those who were not thirsty would not come. The yoke of oxen, the wife, the farm, all drew them away. But those who were thirsty came. "If any man thirsts, let him come." You would take it ill if Christ should not invite you to the dainties of the gospel. Well, do you thirst? Christ invites you. Are you hungry? Will you eat? Will you drink? Christ invites you. The invitation is to thirsters; therefore, get this thirst.

QUESTION. What directions can you give to attain this thirst?

ANSWER. I will give directions, first, to those who have it not; second, to those who have.

For those who have it not, consider something of God, something of the law, something of sin, something of your lives, and something of eternity.

Consider God. Consider the purity, justice, and power of God.

God is a holy God, so pure that His eyes cannot behold iniquity so as to approve of it. See what is said in Psalm 5:4: "For Thou art not a God that hast pleasure in wickedness, neither shall evil dwell with Thee." No unclean thing shall ever enter into His presence. God is a holy God, and who can stand before Him (1 Samuel 6:20)? "He is of purer eyes than to behold iniquity" (Habakkuk 1:13). Well, if God is holy and pure, what will you do who are unholy, impure, wicked, carnal, and corrupt? He is a holy God with whom you have to do.

He is a just God, a God who has said, "The soul that sins shall die." Be he great or small, rich or poor, young or old, learned or unlearned, the soul that sins shall die. In Psalm 143:2 David says, "Enter not into judgment, O Lord, with Thy servant, for no flesh living shall be justified in Thy sight." The Lord is so just, so righteous, so exact that no living flesh can be justified in His sight. Flesh is guilty before God, and sinners must die because God is righteous.

As God is pure and holy, He hates all sin, even the appearance of evil and the thoughts of the heart. As God is just, and will punish sin, so God is powerful to do it. God has a strong arm, and when he comes to

punish sin He can do it to purpose. See what Job said in
Job 16:12: "I was at ease, but He hath broken me asunder. He hath also taken me by my neck, and shaken me
to pieces, and set me up for His mark." Did God deal
thus with holy Job? What, then, will He do with sinners? Is not God a consuming fire? Is not God terrible
in righteousness? Can any escape the hands of God?
You sinners in Zion, can you escape the hands of God?
What will you do in the day of visitation when God
comes? Can you stand out against the Almighty? Can
you plead with God and bring forth arguments to justify
yourselves? God will condemn you. He will shake you to
pieces. God will break your bones.

Now, the consideration of God's purity, of God's justice, and of God's power should make you thirst after
Christ, who can make you holy, and free you from His
justice and power so that He might not destroy you.

Consider the law. In the law of God, in the Ten Com-
mandments, much is forbidden and many things are
commanded. He who is angry without cause, he who
says to his brother, "Raca," or "Thou fool," is in danger
of hell fire. He who looks upon a woman and lusts after
her has committed adultery; and adulterers shall be
shut out of the kingdom of heaven. People often think
that thoughts are free and lust is free from condemnation, but what did Paul say? "When the commandment
came, sin revived and I died; the commandment slew
me." If the law once enters and seizes your heart, it will
drink up the moisture of your spirit; it will make you
restless day and night; it will be as an arrow in your
liver, as a hot, burning iron.

Paul once thought himself blameless, civil, and just,
and believed that no man should be saved sooner than

himself; but he was deceived. When the law came he saw what a sinner he was—what vile thoughts, lusts, and practices he had been guilty of—and the law slew him. The law pronounces a curse over your heads. And James tells you that he who breaks one law is guilty of breaking them all. Do you not see a need for Christ now? Have you no thirsting desires after Christ, who shall deliver you from the law, who shall free you from the curse? If you do not have Christ to do it, you will stand and fall by the law, and you cannot be justified. The Jews would be saved, as it were, by the law, but they perished, seeking righteousness by the law; and so will all who go that way.

Consider sin. Are you not sinners? If there is anyone here who says he is not a sinner, let him depart; but we are all sinners. Let us consider the nature of sin. Oh, how sin defiles us; how sin blackens us! What ugly, loathsome creatures sin makes us! And those who are in their blood, in their filthiness, those who die in their sin, woe to them! Let us, then, lay to heart the evil of sin.

I am persuaded that there is no one here who has any understanding but will see a great deal of evil at one time or another in sin. It is an offense against God; it is the death of the soul; it is the breach of the command. Sin is that which separates God and men.

Now, what you understand conceptually, bring it down and realize it in your hearts; follow it with meditation, and let meditation bring to mind the evil of sin and bring in the indictment: "I am guilty of these many sins." Let conscience sit as judge in you and speak out. Conscience will condemn you and say, "Oh, you have sinned against my Lord and Master. I am His deputy, and I sit as a judge in your soul. I am telling you that you are a damned, lost creature."

Now, when things are brought home thus, then you will thirst after a pardon; then you will look for salvation; then you will see Christ's blood, Christ's intercession, and Christ's merits to be precious. Stout-hearted sinners and highwaymen, when the sentence of death has been pronounced over their heads, and they have seen that they are condemned men, have fallen down upon their knees and begged for mercy. So many stout-hearted sinners, if they would but follow home their sin by meditation, and bring the notion home to their hearts, would see their need of Christ, and to have mercy and grace through Him.

Consider your own lives. Have you any lease of your lives, as Hezekiah had? Do you know whether you shall live another week or year, or another night or day? Are not your lives uncertain? Do we not find in Scripture, and in daily experience, how suddenly men and women are pulled away by some hand of God? Sennacherib's army was smitten all in one night. One hundred eighty-five thousand men, fifty thousand Beth-shemites, smitten for peeping into the ark. Herod was eaten with worms; the Tower of Siloam fell upon eighteen; two bears out of the woods tore forty-two children apart.

And have we not many examples in our own days? How many are blown up with powder? How many are burned with fire? How many drop down in the streets as they go along? Why do you not thirst after Christ and His righteousness? There is no way for you but by Christ; it is Christ alone who will secure your souls. So can you be too early? If Christ is not yours, and you die, woe to you. Christ said that you will die in your sins.

This would be a sad sentence to be pronounced over your head, to be written upon your doors or hearts, that you shall die in your sins. It would have been better if you had never been born. Now, unless you get an interest in Christ, you must die in your sins.

Consider eternity. Here you have a being but for a little time, but what comes next? There is an eternal condition of bliss or woe, and most go the wrong way. There is a possibility for you of eternal happiness, and the way is to thirst after Christ. Sit down and consider with yourself, you who are in the gall of bitterness, and have deluded your soul hitherto with a form of godliness, "Ere long I must go hence, and there are thousands going to hell for every one who goes to heaven. Well, it is time for me to look to myself. I may be gone before the next day, before the next year. Is Christ mine?"

Are you a swearer, a drunkard, a worldling, a whoremaster, one who rails, slanders, and backbites others? Christ is none of yours. The Scriptures are clear: none such shall enter into the kingdom of heaven. Therefore, consider that there is eternal woe for all those who die in their natural condition, who do not have this thirst in them after the Lord Christ and His righteousness. Oh, therefore, give no rest to God, nor any rest to your soul, until you find that you are delivered.

Now to you who are godly, and have some thirst in your souls after Christ: many times you grow lukewarm, flat, dead, and secure. You need to be quickened, and to have your thirst stirred up in you.

To that end, consider your own infirmities. Have you no infirmities? Is there no deadness, dullness, or laziness? How do you perform the worship of God, and the duties thereof? Are you not more carnal than spiritual? Do not your hearts wander? Are you not sleepy? Are you not formal? Do you not many times neglect your duties? Do you not come short? Surely these and many other things you know about yourselves. And where did all these things come from? From the body of sin, from the old man that is in you. Paul was sensible of this. In Romans 7 he found a law in his members warring against the law of his mind. He found that he was carnal, sold under sin. He found that he was unspiritual, and was troubled at this. His thirst was then increased, for what did he say? "O wretched man that I am, who shall deliver me? I thank God through Jesus Christ." He thirsted after Christ, and the coming of Christ to deliver him. In the same way, the serious consideration of your own infirmities and corruptions, and the hindrances, clogs, and obstacles you have from them in your pursuit of Christianity, should cause your thirst to be greater and greater daily.

Consider what work you have to do, and what little strength you have to do it. Christians have a great deal of work to do here in the world: they should pray continually; they should withstand the tempter and all his temptations; they should overcome the world; they should work the works of God; they should side with Christ and His interests, with the gospel, and with the power of godliness. They have their lusts to mortify, and great things to do.

Now, how will you do these? Christ said, "Without Me, you can do nothing." Will you not thirst after Christ now, thirst after strength from Him, assurance from Him, new influences from him, and more of His

Spirit daily? Many act in their own strength, and therefore so little good comes thereof. We pray by our own natural abilities and natural parts, and through power and gifts acquired; and therefore, I say, so little good comes of all. But had we divine strength to pray, and to do all we do—if we went out in His name and in His strength, and worked the works of God—who could stand before us then?

Consider the great good that is to be had by Christ. Have you not wants? Why, there is infinite good to be had by Christ. In Him is all fullness; with Him is plenteous redemption. He has unsearchable riches of grace. He has the residue of the Spirit. He has whatsoever may make our lives comfortable, whatsoever may make our lives happy. Christ has all in His own hands; and therefore you should hunger and thirst after Christ more and more.

Consider what is promised to you by Christ. The promise is that there shall be times of refreshing when Christ comes (Acts 3:19). Then the times of restitution of all things shall come. There are times for these things. And so when the Lamb shall be the Light, then the Lamb shall lead you to the Fountain of living waters; then you shall hunger and thirst no more; then all tears shall be wiped from your eyes. Why do you not thirst after these things, and after the Lord Jesus Christ and His coming? The Spirit says, "Come," and the Bride says, "Come." And what, are your souls asleep? Should we not say, "Come, Lord. Come quickly"? The times in which we live are sad times, but the coming of the Lord would change all, rectify all, and satisfy all. Therefore consider these things, and your thirst after Christ will be increased.

Lastly, if you who thirst would have your thirst more lively and enlarged, remember what sweetness you have found in Christ at some time or other. When men remember that they have drunk fine wine, the very remembrance of it makes them thirst after that wine all the more. When Christ made wine at the marriage feast and brought it forth, the people were so affected with it that they called the governor and asked him why he had kept the best wine until then. So when Christians remember what ravishments they have had from Christ at times, what bursts of joy, what sound peace, what sweet communion with the Father through Him, what outpourings of His Spirit, this will enlarge their hearts and their desires. Some Christians have had large experiences of this sort; they have had flagons of wine to drink, and apples of comfort to feed upon. And the more they remember these, the larger will be their thirstings after Christ.

Christ's Willingness to Save Sinners, Part 1

"Let him that is athirst come."
Revelation 22:17

"Let him that is athirst come." Christ does not say here, "Let him that is athirst seek out," and yet that would have been humane and courteous. Christ does not say, "Let him that is athirst go to Jordan." Christ did not send them to Moses, nor to any of the brooks or cisterns. But Christ said, "Let him that is athirst come." He tells him where he should come, and to what he should come. The meaning is clear: "Let him come to Me. Let him come to Me for drink, for satisfaction; let him that is athirst come." Here are exceeding kindness, choice love, and peculiar mercy. "Come unto Me and drink," is how it is said in John 7:37. "I have drink for him, water of life for him." We see that in the next words: "And whosoever will, let him take of the water of life freely.

What is meant by the word "come"? It does not mean to come bodily, for you all know that is when the body removes from one place and goes to another. But rather it means spiritually. It is not the feet of the body, but the feet of the soul that are required. "Coming" in Scripture means believing. Unbelief is departing from God. Hebrews 3:12: "Take heed, brethren, lest there be in any of you an evil heart of unbelief in departing from the living God." A heart of unbelief is a heart that

127

departs from God and goes away from Him. So in Hebrews 10:38: "The just shall live by faith, but if any man draw back, my soul shall have no pleasure in him." An unbelieving heart is a heart that draws back and departs from God. But to come to God and Christ is to believe.

And this believing is not only an assent unto some truth, an assent that Christ is the Messiah, that Christ is the Savior of the world. No, it is not only to assent, for devils believe in that sense, and even Antichrist believes then; indeed, many who perish believe, for they assent to such truths.

Neither is it an assurance, as some call faith a full or thorough persuasion of the heart that such and such is true. No, assurance is not faith. Assurance is a consequence or effect of faith, and not of the nature and essence of faith. Many shall be saved who never had assurance, and many are justified who have no assurance. What, then, is this faith? What is this "coming"?

There is assent unto truth, assent unto Scripture, which is in the understanding; and so is assurance, for we speak of "assurance of understanding." But faith is in the understanding, and in the will also, when, upon clear understanding of a truth, the will comes to choose and close with that truth.

This is to believe. Some call it "resting," some "rolling," some "depending" or "relying." All these are metaphoric expressions; but if you will have it in the proper nature and sense, faith is the assent of the understanding to truth and unto Christ, and the will's choosing of Christ. It chooses Christ for its righteousness, for its salvation, for grace, for life, for peace, for all. This is "coming," when the will puts forth an act that carries forth the soul to choose Christ.

So, then, Christ says, "Let him that is athirst come." And by this it would seem that there is a power in man to come.

What power was there in Lazarus to come forth from the grave when Christ said, "Lazarus, come forth"? There was as much power in Lazarus then as there is in man now to come to Christ when He says, "Come." There was none in Lazarus to come forth; neither is there any in man naturally to believe. In John 6:44, Christ said, "No man can come to Me except the Father which hath sent Me draw him."

What is the drawing of the Father? Some say that it is a thirsting begotten in the soul; but surely that cannot be, for Christ said, "Let him that is athirst come." A man may be thirsty and yet not come to Christ. But this drawing of the Father is a working of that power in the soul that goes out to Christ. It may see a need for Christ because of sin, wrath, and the like, yet till God works a power in the soul to go out to Christ, it does not come to Christ. And therefore you find in John 6:44, "No man can come to Me except the Father which hath sent Me draw him." God's drawing in verse 65 is said to be God's gift: "Therefore I said unto you that no man can come unto Me except it were given unto him of the Father," that is, "unless God gives him the power to come unto Me." So the Father's drawing is putting that virtue and power into a thirsty soul so as to close with Christ.

OBJECTION. But surely these invitations are in vain if a man cannot come when he is invited. To what end are they?

ANSWER. The sun shines upon the rock, and the rain falls down upon the rocks, yet no man expects that the sun should melt the rocks or that the rain should make the rocks fruitful. But the adjacent parts and fields have the benefit; and so, though invitations fall upon rocks, yet the other persons may have the benefit.

Also, generally in these invitations the Lord conveys His power; the Lord works this faith in their souls and gives them the power to close with Christ. Lazarus came forth; together with the invitation, Lazarus was given power to come forth. Ezekiel 2:1: "And he said unto me, 'Son of Man, stand upon thy feet, and I will speak unto thee.' " Mark it, "and the Spirit entered into me when he spoke unto me, and set me upon my feet." Ezekiel was so smitten with the sight of glory that he was not able to rise. He was told to stand, but he could not. And then the Spirit entered into him and set him upon his feet. So when Christ says here, "Come," by Christ's speaking the Spirit may be, and many times is, conveyed, and causes a man to come. There is that life, that grace communicated to the soul, together with the invitation, that makes a man do the thing, and enables him thereunto. So invitations are not in vain. And so much for the opening of the word "come."

The doctrinal point I shall commend to you is this:

DOCTRINE: The Lord Christ is very desirous that sinners, thirsty sinners, should come to Him for relief, that they should be saved, that they should have refreshing virtue from Him—grace, pardon, peace, and whatsoever will do their souls good. "Let him that is athirst come."

Now because it lies in the hearts of all sinners to question the willingness of God and Christ to save them and do them good, therefore I shall insist the more upon this, and make it out fully to you.

The leper in the gospel said, "Master, if Thou wilt, Thou canst make me clean." We can hear him saying, "I know Thou hast power, but if Thou *wilt* or not, there lies the stick." And here lies that which sticks with sinners, to question the willingness of God and Christ. Now Christ is very willing that sinners should come unto Him, and this I shall make out in several ways.

1. From the consideration of Christ's laying down His greatness and His glory, which would daunt and discourage sinners. When a judge comes into the country with his greatness, it makes delinquents and malefactors afraid; but now Christ lays down His majesty, His greatness and glory, and whatseover is dreadful and terrible unto us. John 17:5: "And now, O Father, glorify Thou Me with Thine own self, with the glory which I had with Thee before the world was." Christ had laid aside His glory when He came down into the world. He came in the form of a servant, in a low and mean condition.

When a prince lays aside his greatness, and comes and converses with beggars and sinners, then they can more freely come unto him and speak to him. The Lord Jesus Christ laid aside His glory and greatness, and came and conversed with sinners here in the world, which is a great argument that He was willing to do sinners good, and that they should come unto Him and be saved by Him.

2. Consider how the Lord Christ has fitted Himself to relieve sinners. Christ has endured a great deal of hardship, suffered heavy things, and trod the winepress of His Father's wrath alone. Corn that makes bread and drink endures the heat and the cold, enduring the slate and the mill where it is ground; and so the bread and

drink are made thereof.

The Lord has endured all that the Father required of Him so that He might be the bread of life and the water of life to us. He has suffered bitter things, an accursed death. In Luke 12:50 Christ said, "I have a baptism to be baptized with, and how I am straitened till it be accomplished." It is as if He had said, "I thirst to lay down My blood so that it may be drink for the world. As much as any in the world thirsts for my blood, and to drink of it, I do more than all the world." The Lord Jesus had suffered circumcision. He had suffered whipping, being crowned with thorns, being spat upon, reproaches, revilings, cursings, the displeasure of His Father, desertions, and temptations by Satan, and all that He might be fit to save us, that He might be bread and drink for us, relief for us. Is not Christ willing that you should eat of His flesh and drink of His blood? Is He not willing that you should come to Him and have the benefit of His sufferings? "I am distressed," He said, "till it is accomplished." Upon the cross, Christ said, "I thirst." And now it is finished.

3. From the very end of Christ's coming it is evident that Christ is very willing and desirous that sinners should come unto Him, and be saved and refreshed by Him. What was the end of Christ's coming? Matthew 18:11: "For the Son of Man is come to save that which was lost." Were not all lost in Adam? Are not all under the curse of the law? Are not all children of wrath by nature? Are not all enemies of God through wicked works in their minds? The end of Christ's coming was to save that which was lost. In Luke 19:10 it is expressed even more fully: "For the Son of Man is come to seek and to save that which is lost." It might have been said,

"It's true, Christ will save those who are lost if they will come to Him." But Christ has come to *seek them out,* and to save that which is lost. This is the Good Shepherd who goes and seeks out the lost sheep, and takes it upon His shoulders and brings it home. When a shepherd's sheep are scattered—some in one lane, some upon one common, some in one field, some in another—he goes and seeks out the sheep and brings them home. So the Lord Christ came for that very end: to seek out and to save that which was lost. Are you a poor, thirsty, sinful soul? Are you lost in your own apprehension? Are you at the gates of death and hell? The Lord Christ came to save you, to seek you out. He is willing, forward and ready to do it. He came for that very end.

4. Christ's willingness and readiness to do this work will appear if you consider the cures that he wrought when He was here in the world. Did not Christ heal all diseases? Did He not heal the blind, the lame, the sick, the dumb, the deaf, those possessed with devils? Did not Christ show compassion towards them all and heal them? Matthew 4:23–24: "And Jesus went about all Galilee, teaching in their synagogues, and preaching the gospel of the kingdom, and healing all manner of sickness, and all manner of diseases among the people. And His fame went through all Syria, and they brought unto Him all sick people that were taken with divers diseases and torments, and those which were possessed with devils, and those which were lunatic, and those which had the palsy, and He healed them."

Is not Christ willing and ready to do good to sinners? He does not forbid them to come to Him, let the disease be what it will, and the diseased party be what he will. And it is thought that when Christ healed their bodies, He healed their souls too. Christ healed all diseases. In Matthew 8 you have three remarkable instances. A leper came to Christ and said, "Lord, if Thou wilt, Thou canst make me clean." He did not come believing, but rather doubting.

What followed? "Jesus put forth His hand and touched him, saying, 'I will; be thou clean.' " "Why do you question My will?" said Christ. "I am more willing to heal you than you are desirous of it. I will," said He, be thou clean." Christ immediately showed His willingness and cured the man with a word and a touch.

Later in that chapter there came to Him a centurion, who solicited Him on behalf of his servant, saying, "Master, speak the word only and my servant shall be healed." Christ said, "I have not found so great faith, no, not in Israel, as in this centurion." And in verse 13 Christ said, "Go thy way, and as thou hast believed, so be it unto thee." Here Christ healed one with but a word.

And then He came to Peter's house. There Peter's mother-in-law lay sick with a fever. Christ touched her hand and the fever left her. Christ but touched her hand and said nothing, and yet the fever left her. Christ is willing to cure sinners; and He can easily do it with a word, or with a word and a touch, or with a touch alone.

Christ is so forward that before it is even desired He does it. In John 5:6, when Jesus saw the impotent man there, knowing that he had been a long time in that state, He said to him, "Wilt thou be made whole?" The man did not ask if Christ would heal him. Rather, Christ came and found him, and said, "Wilt thou be made whole?" The man then responded, "O Sir, I have none to put me in; when the angel stirs another steps in before me." To which Christ said, "Take up thy bed and walk." Christ asked him the question, listened to his complaint, and then healed him. Oh! Christ is willing to do sinners good, and to save sinners!

5. This appears from the commands of Christ. When a thing is commanded, those who command would fain have it done. Now, the Lord Christ commands men to come unto Him. He commands them to believe. John 14:1: "Let not your hearts be troubled; ye believe in God, believe also in Me."

"Believe in Me": there's ease, rest, refreshment, deliverance, and salvation for you. And 1 John 3:23: "This is His commandment, that we should believe in the name of His Son Jesus Christ." The Father commands that we should believe in the name of His Son, the Lord Jesus Christ; and it is the commandment of the Son that we believe in Him.

When the father commanded his son to go to the vineyard and dig there, the father was very willing that the child should go and do it. And so when God the Father and Christ the Son command us to believe, they are very willing that we should do so. When princes send out their commands to the people to do such and such things, they are very desirous that they should be done. So when God gives out His commands in the gospel, and when Christ commands men in the gospel to come, it is an argument that there is a strong will in Him for it to happen.

6. Does not Christ sweetly invite you, and use sweet invitations and allurements to draw sinners to Him? Can there be sweeter invitations than what you have from Christ upon this account in Matthew 11:28: "Come

unto Me, all ye that are weary and heavy laden, and I will give you rest"?

Can you hear Christ crying out, "Oh, you poor sinners of the world, you poor sinners of the earth, you who travail under the burden of your sins, you who are heavy laden, you who are ready to sink into hell through fear of wrath: come unto Me; come unto Me." He does not say, "Why have you broken Moses' law? Why have you offended My Father? Why have you lived so basely and vilely?" No, He says, "Come unto Me, you who are weary and heavy laden, you who are ready to sink and perish, who are hungry and thirsty and know not which way to turn for relief; come unto Me."

See what a blessed invitation is given in Isaiah 55: 1–2: "Ho, everyone that thirsteth, come ye to the waters, and he that hath no money, come ye, buy and eat; yea, come buy wine and milk without money and without price. Wherefore do you lay out your money for that which is not bread, and your labor for that which satisfieth not? Hearken diligently unto Me, and eat ye that which is good, and let your soul delight itself in fatness." Is not here a sweet, gracious, blessed invitation to poor sinners, unto such as we are here this day? The Lord Christ is speaking unto you this day: "Ho, everyone, everyone who thirsts, young or old, rich or poor, learned or unlearned, of whatsoever condition you are—are you thirsty? Would you have mercy, peace, grace, and the Spirit of Christ? Would you have anything to do your souls good? Then come, come unto Me. Come to the waters."

"Aye, but I have no money!"

It matters not; come without money. Come, for here is wine, milk, bread, marrow, and fatness; there's that which will make your souls live; here's virtue in Christ to make your souls live forever. So we read in Proverbs 23:26: "My son, give me thy heart." God says, "O my son, give Me your heart." Christ is the everlasting Father and He says, "My son, give Me your heart. Come to me."

Another passage worth observing is Revelation 3:20: "Behold, I stand at the door and knock; if any man hear My voice and open the door, I will come in to him and will sup with him, and he with Me." It is as if He had said, "Behold, I stand at the door and knock. I came down from heaven into My ordinances. I knock at the door of your hearts and consciences; if any man will open now, if any man would have water of life from Me, if any man would have bread of life from Me, if any man would have communion with Me, let him but open and receive Me in, and I will sup with him and he with Me." What sweet invitations have we from Christ! How forward, how ready is the Lord Jesus to do poor sinners good!

7. It appears in that the Lord Christ has instituted and appointed His officers, His messengers, His ministers, and sent them to woo, entreat, beseech, and draw men unto Him. The Lord has set up in the Church officers whose purpose is to make known His forwardness and readiness to receive sinners, and to go forth in His name, and to get them to come to Christ. It is our work to beseech you, brethren, and to entreat you to hearken to the Lord Christ, to come in to Him, to come and taste of His dainties, to receive righteousness, grace, strength, salvation, and pardon. This is our work: to get men into Christ, to fetch you into the fold. Luke 14:16–17: "A certain man made a great supper, and bade many, and sent his servants at supper time to say unto

them that were bidden, 'Come, for all things are now ready.' " Christ is the great man, and He makes a supper in the time of the gospel. He sends out His servants. He sends out the ministers to invite and call men, saying, "Supper is ready; all things are ready." Christ has satisfied divine justice. He has laid down His life and shed His blood. He has risen from the dead. He has overcome the world, overcome the devil, and opened heaven. All things are ready for you to feed upon.

The passage continues: "Then the master of the house, being angry, said to his servants, 'Go out quickly into the streets and lanes of the city, and bring in hither the poor and the maimed, the lame and the blind.' And the servants said, 'Lord, it is done as thou hast commanded, and yet there is room.' And the Lord said unto his servants, 'Go out into the highways and hedges, and compel them to come in that my house may be filled.' " He said, "Go! My apostles, My disciples, My ministers, My servants, go fetch in men and women from highways and hedges, from lanes and streets, from all parts. Oh, bring them into the gospel; bring them into My house; bring them into the kingdom of heaven. Tell them of the dainties there; tell them of the danger abroad. This is the great work of the ministry."

This is a clear demonstration that the Lord Christ would have sinners saved. He would have His house filled. He stands not upon what they are. "Let them be blind, maimed, naked, poor, or wounded; bring them in," says Christ. "Let them taste the dainties of the gospel; let them hear of mercy through Me, of pardon and forgiveness in Me."

Proverbs 9:1–6: "Wisdom hath built her house. She hath hewn out her seven pillars. She hath killed her beasts; she hath mingled her wine; she hath also furnished her table; she hath sent forth her maidens; she crieth upon the highest places of the city, 'Whoso is simple, let him come in hither.' As for him that lacketh understanding, she saith to him, 'Come, eat of my bread and drink of the wine that I have mingled. Forsake the foolish and live, and go in the way of understanding.' " This is spoken of Christ and the times of the gospel. The ministers are said to be maidens who are sent forth to allure and draw poor souls in to Jesus Christ. So the great work of the ministry is to make known the willingness of Christ, and to bring sinners unto Christ so that they may have mercy from Him.

2 Corinthians 5:19–20: "God was in Christ, reconciling the world to Himself, not imputing their trespasses unto them, and hath committed unto us the word of reconciliation. Now then, we are ambassadors for Christ, as though God did beseech you by us; we pray ye in Christ's stead, be ye reconciled to God." Paul is saying, "I am an ambassador of God, and God beseeches you by us. God beseeches sinners, and therefore we beseech you. We beseech you for the Lord's sake to be reconciled to God."

Do not stand out from God and Christ any longer, but come in to God; come in to Christ. And so God will receive you and Christ will receive you. God beseeches you by ministers. God entreats you. The commission was: "Go, teach all nations." He commands us to teach all nations and to acquaint men with the riches of grace by Christ, with the wonderful love and kindness of God in Christ, with what's to be had by Christ, so that people might come to Him and have mercy and relief from Him.

8. This willingness of Christ to do sinners good will appear yet further in that He accepts the least and lowest degrees of faith, and will not discourage the weakest soul that comes to Him. Matthew 12:20: "A bruised reed shall He not break, and smoking flax shall He not quench, till He send forth judgment unto victory." Christ will be very tender with a bruised reed, very tender with a smoking flax. He will not break one; He will not quench the other. He will not deal harshly and roughly with them, but He will send forth judgment unto victory. He will give them power over all their corruptions, over all their fears and doubts. He will enable them to judge all their enemies and be victorious over them.

So it is that we read in Isaiah 45:22, "Look unto Me and be ye saved, all the ends of the earth." Christ is saying, "If I have but a good look from you, I will entertain you. Look unto Me but with the weakest eye of faith. Though it is a dim eye, though it is but half an eye, look unto Me and be saved." And Isaiah 40:11: "He shall feed His flock like a shepherd. He shall gather the lambs with His arms, and carry them in His bosom, and shall gently lead those that are with young." See how tender the Lord Christ, the Good Shepherd, will be with those who are weak. He will gather the lambs with His arms, as a shepherd does when he goes abroad. When a lamb is newborn, it is weak and feeble; and when the weather is cold and frosty he takes the lamb up in his arms and carries it home and gives it milk. So the Lord will deal with a poor, weak, feeble soul: He will carry it in the arms of His providence, in the arms of His Spirit, in those everlasting arms of His that never fail. He will carry the lambs in His bosom, and gently lead those who are with young. Thus He deals with them. Hence Paul says in Romans 14:1, "Him that is weak in the faith receive ye, but not to doubtful disputations." Receive him who is weak in the faith. If there is never so little faith, receive him; if there is but one dram of faith, receive him.

9. The willingness of the Lord Christ to do sinners good appears in that He does not shut up this water of life, though He knows that but few will come to Him for it, and that those who do come to Him often abase it and Him too. People hasten more to the waters for their bodies, to the baths, to epsom, and to new drinks that they now have; they flock to have these for the body, and can magnify them and speak wonderfully well of them. But few come to Christ; and when they do come they will hardly drink. They speak evil of those doctrines He gives them: "These are hard sayings!"

Peter himself denied Christ once, twice, three times. Thus Christ is dealt with by sinners, and, notwithstanding all this, Christ does not shut up or lock up the water, but the waters stand open for any to come. Let whosoever will come; let him come and drink of the waters of life freely. If Christ did not have a mind that we should have these waters, He would have taken a course to deprive us of them. He could easily dry up the waters, dry up the gospel. But the waters are not dried up; they are not taken from us; there is freedom for any to come, notwithstanding that they have abused the waters.

10. It is strong evidence that the Lord Christ is willing to save sinners and to do them good in that He is grieved, troubled, and affected greatly that sinners will not come to Him for these waters. Luke 13:34; 19:42: "O

Jerusalem, Jerusalem," said Christ, weeping over her, "how oft would I have gathered thee as a hen doth her chickens, and ye would not. O Jerusalem, Jerusalem, that thou hadst known in this day the things which belong unto thy peace, but now they are hidden from thine eyes." Christ is grieved to the heart that men and women do not come to Him. Though they have no money, though they have nothing to buy the water with, yet that they will not come and even fetch the water—this grieves Christ and troubles Him to the very heart. Oh, that these public places should be so empty upon a Lord's day, so empty upon a weekday! There's water of life, and none will come and drink the water! "How often, how often," may Christ say, "would I have saved such a town, such a nation, such a people, and they would not!" Christ weeps over souls, families, and cities.

11. It is wonderfully perspicuous and clear that Christ would do sinners good in that He presses them with the strongest arguments there can be to partake of the good that is to be had by Himself. What promises does He make, what evils does He threaten! There are two great arguments that prevail with all the world, yet will not prevail here. He sets life and death before men: "If you will come, here's life for you. If you will not come, you are dead men." People will not keep within doors when these are the arguments. "My life is at stake, and if I go I am a madman; if not I am a lost and undone man."

Christ says, "Why will ye die, O house of Israel? I am not willing that you should die. Why will you die? Why will you die? Turn to Me and live. Come to Me and live." It is what He said in Isaiah 55:3: "Incline your ear and come unto Me. Hear and your souls shall live, and I will make an everlasting covenant with you, even the sure mercies of David." Is not here encouragement enough now to come to Christ? "Incline your ear and come to Me, and your souls shall live and you shall have everlasting mercies and everlasting comforts." John 3:16: "For God so loved the world that He gave His only begotten Son, that whosoever believeth in Him should not perish, but have everlasting life."

Here's life and death set before you. Come, you poor sinner, and believe in the Lord Jesus; close with Him. Here's life for you, everlasting life for you. Refuse to do it, and there's everlasting death for you; you shall perish. How peremptory is the Lord here. Mark 16:15–16: "Go ye into all the world and preach the gospel to every creature; he that believeth and is baptized shall be saved, but he that believeth not shall be damned." How all-encompassing is the gospel. "He that believeth," meaning he who comes to Christ, shall be saved—saved from all his sin, saved from the power of death, saved from the wrath of God, saved from hellfire, saved from the guilt of his own conscience.

"But he that believeth not shall be damned." How He presses men to come to Him! If there is any weight in heaven or hell, it's all laid upon your coming to Christ or refusing Him. If you come to Christ, all heaven is yours; all the glory, all the joy, all the comfort, all the blessings, all the happiness there is yours. If you will not come to Christ, all the terrors of hell are yours: all the darkness, all the mournings, all the howlings, all the gnashings of teeth, all the misery there will be yours. Therefore, see how willing the Lord Jesus is that sinners should come, and that they should be saved.

Christ's Willingness to Save Sinners, Part 2

"Let him that is athirst come."
Revelation 22:17

12. Another evidence of Christ's willingness to save sinners who will come unto Him is that the Lord ventures and hazards losing many by making known His free grace and willingness to save sinners; for when sinners hear that Christ is willing to save them, and very desirous also, many abuse His free grace, His rich mercy, and His willingness to do their souls good. "If Christ is so willing," they say, "we will stay awhile; it will suffice hereafter." Jude 4 says that they turn grace into wantonness. When sinners hear that Christ died and shed His blood for sinners, that He is willing that sinners should come in, that He waits for them, and that He entreats and presses them to come to Him, they take advantage of this to sin more freely, to hold out to the uttermost. And thus the Lord runs a hazard of losing many by making known the riches of His grace, the freedom of His mercy and loving-kindness, which shows a very strong desire in Christ to save sinners.

13. It is evident that Christ is very desirous of the salvation of sinners in that He takes sinners when they are in the worst state of all, at the height of wickedness. If a prince will take into his family those who are sick from the plague of leprosy, it is an argument that he has a mind to have them live in his family, and that he is

desirous of their company.

The Lord Jesus Christ takes sinners when they are at their very worst. Saul was at the height of his blasphemy, at the height of murder, at the height of persecution; and Christ said, "Saul, Saul, why persecutest thou Me? Thy blasphemies rage, and thy persecutions have come up to heaven." In 1 Timothy 1 Paul wrote that he was a persecutor, a blasphemer, and an injurious person, but yet he said that he obtained mercy. Even when he was so great and notorious a sinner, Christ came and took him in.

It is an argument, then, that Christ is very desirous of the salvation of sinners that He will take sinners when they are in the height of their wickedness. The prodigal had run from his father's house, and had spent years in wicked practices, in whoredom, drunkenness, gaming, and running in the ways of the world. Now when he was in this height of wickedness, it pleased God and Christ to call him, to bring him home, and to receive him again. Had not Christ been desirous of the salvation of sinners, He might have shut the door against the prodigal and said, "You shall never come indoors again." Had not the Father been desirous for the Son's sake to save sinners, He would not have entertained the prodigal. This is not a wish without any effort behind it, but a strong, efficacious desire in God and Christ to save sinners.

When the Jews were at their worst, when they had put that innocent One to death, when they had said, "His blood be upon us and upon our children," when they had mocked Him, reviled Him, and accused Him—even after all this Christ took in many of them. Three thousand of them were converted at one of

Peter's sermons by these words: "Him whom ye have crucified with bloody hands hath God raised." Here is a clear evidence of the earnest desire of the Lord Jesus to save sinners. He takes them when they are at their worst, when they have done the uttermost mischief and spite they can against Him and His ways.

14. It is an argument that the Lord Jesus is very desirous of saving sinners if you consider that the Lord takes sinners at the last moment, at the end of their days, when they have no time left to serve Him. He takes them at the very first entreaty and begging for mercy. The thief who had lived wickedly all his days, when he was nailed to the cross and ready to breathe out his last breath, said, "Lord, remember me when Thou comest into Thy kingdom." Christ might have said, "Remember you? Why should I remember you? You have been a bloody wretch, a thief and murderer all your days; and you deserve nothing now but death and damnation!" No, Christ did not say this, but rather, "This day shalt thou be with Me in paradise." There was no time left for the thief to honor and to serve Christ, as he now entreated this favor of Him. And Christ said in reply, "This day shalt thou be with Me in paradise."

Doubtless, though we have but this one instance, and so men should not presume to put off repentance till it is too late, yet I do believe that many a soul has met with mercy when it has been at the gates of death. I say, many poor souls have been burdened with sin, afflicted in conscience and ready to sink, in the gates of death have looked up to Christ and entreated Him to remember them. And Christ has shown them mercy, which shows the forwardness and willingness of Christ to save sinners.

Yet let not any presume to do so, for it is likely that late repentance is seldom true repentance. A deathbed repentance is usually a dead repentance. When it is a fear of hell that shall drive men to look after heaven, they may thank hell for looking after God and Christ. But that is another matter.

15. Last, it is clearly evident that the Lord Christ has a strong inclination to save sinners by His giving out the Scripture in the way and manner He has done. The Lord has given out Scripture so as to answer the objections of men and women, to answer all the cavils of their hearts, all the pleas of corruption and a guilty conscience, and even of the devil himself. The Lord has given Scripture so as to answer all who might hinder others from coming to Him. Matthew 12:31 tells us that "all manner of sins and blasphemies shall be forgiven unto men." What has a sinful heart to say here? What can you object against this? He says that *all manner* of sins and blasphemies shall be forgiven. Are your sins beyond blasphemy? Are they such as do not come within the compass of "all manner of sin"? Let your sins be slight or great, let them be old or new, let them be against law, against gospel, against promises—all manner of sins shall be forgiven. Christ said, though, that "the sin against the Holy Ghost shall not be forgiven." But if you have a heart to look to Christ for mercy, it's an argument that you are free from that sin; for where that sin is, there is impenitence, hardness of heart, and no thinking of repentance or coming to God. But "all manner of sins and blasphemies shall be forgiven." Is not here encouragement enough to poor sinners? So in the next words: "Whosoever will, let him come and drink of the water of life freely." It is laid

down so as to answer all your objections, and to take away all the pleas you have to keep you from Christ. So, then, you see clear evidences that Christ is willing to save sinners.

QUESTION. But why is Christ so willing to save sinners?

ANSWER. First, from His own experience and sense of what it is to be under the displeasure of God. He was once tempted; He was once forsaken; He cried out in that condition, and He knew what the wrath and displeasure of God meant. And now, being full of compassion, He pities all those who are under the disfavor of God. He knows sinners have broken the law, deserving the curse, the wrath of God, eternal death; and now, His compassions being stirred within Him, His bowels yearn and He desires that sinners may come to Him. If anyone thirsts, let him come, let him come. That person shall be freed from the wrath of God, from the curse of the law, from guilt and condemnation. Christ has said, "It's a sad condition, and I am sensible of it. I was in the share and circle of sinners, and I know what it is to be in such a condition."

Second, Christ is so desirous to save sinners so that He may see the travail of His own soul, and that men may see that the end of His coming to save sinners was real; for if Christ's end was to seek and save that which was lost, unless He desires it and uses means to save them, you may say it was not real. Therefore Christ, to make it clear that it really was His end, and that He might see the travail of His soul in suffering, desires that sinners may come in. He invites them extraordinarily and ordinarily. He calls upon them, and would have sinners come to Him to be saved.

Third, Christ does this so that the freeness of God's grace and love may appear and be magnified. Christ is wonderfully desirous that sinners should come in; and when they do come in, they will magnify the riches of grace. Then they will stand and wonder at the love of God and Christ, and that He should wait upon them, beseeching and entreating them to come and accept His mercy and favor.

Application

We may see here that the way of the Lord Christ is for sinners to come in to Him and the Father freely. "Whosoever is athirst, let him come." He does not say, "Let him be compelled to come," or "let him be forced to come," but "let him come." He holds out such riches of grace and mercy, such treasures and excellencies, that certainly, if a soul will but consider and weigh them, it will come. Christ Himself came freely to us, and He would have us come freely to Him. There is no forcing in the act of conversion, but all is free. Though God puts forth a mighty power in the hearts of people, yet He overcomes them with sweetness and loving-kindness. "Let him that is athirst come."

OBJECTION. But people are bidden in Luke 14:23 to "compel them to come in."

ANSWER. This is not an outward compulsion. He does not speak of compulsion by force of arms, but of compelling with force of argument. Propound unto people such motives in the gospel as may compel them to come in; tell them of the beauty of holiness; tell them of the riches of grace; tell them of the love of God and Christ; tell them of the pardon of sins, and answer their objections. There's no forcing in the work of grace, no forcing men to come to God and Christ; but it's all a free work. God draws, but he draws with cords of love. He does not carry men against their wills to Christ, nor does He force them to believe in Him. No, but He sweetens their wills, and overcomes them with kindness and truth; and the majesty, glory, and loveliness of truth overcome their wills so that men come willingly to Christ.

Since Christ is desirous that sinners come to Him, let us not go to any other. Many seek out others, and say with those in Psalm 4:6, "Who will show us any good?" There is no relief for poor sinners in any other but Christ. There is no relief in running to Moses, or David, or prophets, nor to any but Christ—not friends, not honors, not riches, not gifts and talents, not anything in the creature can relieve a thirsty soul but Christ. "If any man thirsts, let him come."

Come to Christ. All other things proclaim to you that it is not in them. The wedge of gold says, "It is not in me." House and land say, "It is not in us." The ships on the sea say, "It is not in us." And all other creatures say the same. It is only in Jesus Christ to relieve a poor soul. Matthew 11:28: "Come unto Me, all ye that are weary and heavy laden, and I will give you rest." He does not say that mountains can refresh you, that angels can refresh you, or that any other creature can refresh you, but it is "Come unto *Me*, all ye that are weary and heavy laden, and *I* will give you rest."

All the virtue that refreshes a guilty soul, a thirsty soul, a sinful soul, all that virtue is in the Lord Jesus Christ. He is the water of life. He is a fountain of living water. He has that to give you which will do your souls good. He can give you His blood to quench the fire of hell, to purge away your guilt, to remove wrath to come. It is in Christ and none other. Therefore, all those who go to others forsake their own mercies and embrace lying vanities; but those who come to Christ go the right way.

Does Christ invite us to come unto Him? Then let us examine and make inquiry whether we have come to Christ or not. I believe there are hardly any under this roof who do not think they have come to Christ, that they are true Christians. And it is worth the inquiry to resolve this case so that we may not be deceived; for Christ said in Matthew 7:22 that "many shall say, 'Lord, Lord,' have we not done thus and so in Thy presence?" But Christ shall say to them, "Depart from Me, I never knew you. You never came to Me." I say, then, it may be worth our time to make inquiry after this case of conscience, whether we have come to Christ or not. And I shall clear it up for you in a few particulars.

1. The soul that has truly come to Christ has seen a sufficiency in Christ to relieve it in every way, and such a sufficiency as has caused it to venture itself upon the Lord Jesus Christ alone and nothing else. Now apply this to your own souls. Have you ever seen such sufficiency in the Lord Jesus as heaven and earth besides do not have? Have you seen such as will make you come off from all and venture upon Him alone? If you have clearly seen the sufficiency of Christ, then your own righteousness is nothing to you. Your own civility, morality, and honesty are as nothing; though they are good in regard to men, yet they are nothing in regard to God and in regard to your souls.

You see an all-sufficiency in Jesus Christ, and an

utter insufficiency in yourselves. "Alas, what's my righteousness," says the soul that has come to Christ. "My righteousness is filthiness, and all that I can ever do is unprofitable before God. Though I have learning, wisdom, gifts, memory, utterance, riches, honors, a calling, and do good in my place, alas, all these things are nothing! I count them as dung. But there's an all-sufficiency in Christ. I have these other things, but these will only damn me and send me to hell."

Take these matters to heart, for it's ill to be deceived in matters of eternity. Have you seen such a sufficiency in the Lord Jesus of wisdom and strength, of righteousness? Have you laid down all your own ability and seen it as nothing? Have you ventured your souls nakedly upon Jesus Christ? Isaiah 45:23–25: "Verily shall one say, 'In the Lord have I righteousness and strength.' " It is a prophecy of the last times concerning Christ: "I have sworn by Myself, the word is gone out of My mouth in righteousness, and it shall not return; that unto Me every knee shall bown, every tongue shall swear." It is spoken of Christ, and applied to Him in Philippians. Surely shall one say, "In the Lord have I righteousness and strength," and even to Him shall men come. Mark it: "In the Lord shall all the seed of Israel be justified and shall glory." Unto Him shall they come. "And all that are incensed against Him shall be ashamed."

"What? Go to Christ?" says one. "There's nothing in Christ." Men speak blasphemously and basely of Christ in these days, but they shall be ashamed. "But unto *Him* shall men come, and in the Lord shall all the seed of Israel be justified and shall glory." They shall be justified in Christ. Therefore, deal truthfully with your own

hearts herein. Be taken off from your own righteousness; build wholly upon Christ. Those who come to
Him do so.

2. The soul that has come to Christ stays itself upon
Him, rests upon Him, and does not go out from Him.
As it ventures itself upon Christ, so it rests content with
Christ. When a woman has chosen a man for her husband, she rests content in him above all the men in the
world. And the soul that has chosen Christ, that comes
to Christ, and believes in Christ in truth rests content
with the Lord Jesus above all in heaven and earth. In
John 6:67 Jesus puts a question to Peter: "Jesus said unto
the twelve, 'Will ye also go away?' Then Simon Peter answered Him, 'Lord, to whom shall we go? Thou hast the
words of eternal life.' " It is as if Peter said, "We are satisfied with Thee. We rest content with Thee. We do not
look beyond Thee. We have enough in Thee and from
Thee to bring us to eternal life." Thus a soul that has
truly come to Christ will join nothing with Christ, but
rests satisfied with Him alone. Try yourselves by this.

3. A soul that has come to Christ in truth accepts the
Lord Jesus Christ upon His own terms. Many will accept
Christ, but it will be on their terms. "I can have Christ
and the world," says one. "I will be content to be a
Christian so long as I can have Christ and my honors,"
says another." A third says, "As long as I can have Christ
and still have my lusts satisfied, and enjoy them, I will
have Christ." And yet a fourth man says, "If I can live
and take my ease and still go to heaven, I will have
Christ." Thus men will have Christ upon their own
terms. But the soul that is thirsty and comes to Christ
in truth takes the Lord Christ upon His own terms. "If
any man," said Christ, "will be My disciple, he must

deny himself and take up his cross" (Matthew 16:24).

These are Christ's terms. A man must lay aside his own wisdom; a man must be content to bear a cross, to meet with reproaches, prison, temptations, persecutions, hard measures—Christ and a cross, Christ and prison, Christ and hunger and nakedness, and whatever temptations God wills. "For we are slain all the day long for Thy sake," we are told in Romans 8:36. So a soul that comes to Christ in truth takes Christ upon His own terms. Christ and mortification of your lusts, Christ and death to the world, Christ and death to sin: these all go together. Men would have Christ and live for the world, live for sin, live for vanity; but these cannot stand together. He who is Christ's has crucified the flesh with the affections and lusts thereof; he has crucified them, and accepts Christ upon His own terms.

4. Where the soul truly comes to Christ and closes with Him, there it gives itself up to Christ to dispose of it. When a woman is married, she leaves the house of her father and mother and gives herself up to be guided by her husband. Therefore in Psalm 45:10–11 it says, "Hearken, O daughter, and consider, and incline thine ear. Forget also thine own people and thy father's house; so shall the king greatly desire thy beauty. For he is thy Lord, and worship thou Him." So a soul gives itself up to Christ and forgets all former engagements, former customs, practices, and ways it walked in, and gives itself up to be ruled now by Christ and by His laws. Says the soul, "I am now come into a King's family. I am come into a great court. I must now be ruled by the laws of this King, by the laws of His house." And therefore it is that Christ says, "My sheep hear My voice." If I am one who is in the fold of Christ, if I am a sheep of Christ, I

will hear His voice. A stranger I will not hear; a stranger I will not follow.

Now, how is it with you? Do you follow the voice of the world, of the flesh, of hell? If so, you have not given yourselves up to Christ; for if you had you would follow Him and hear Him, and not strangers. In Revelation 14:4, the 144,000 "follow the Lamb whithersoever He goeth." They do not follow the lions of the world, but they follow the Lamb wherever He goes. Christ is their Head; Christ is their Lord; Christ is their Guide. So the soul that comes to Christ is guided and led by Christ; it follows Christ. Try yourselves by this.

5. A soul that has come to Christ in truth is daily made more and more like Him. Once it comes to Christ, the soul sees such beauty, such glory, such excellence in Christ, such wisdom in Christ, that it is willing to be conformed to Christ in everything. Such a soul says, "Not my will, but Thine, Lord Jesus; not my thoughts, but Thy thoughts." Paul said that we have the very mind of Christ, and not only the mind of Christ but the life of Christ. Galatians 2:20: "I live not, but Christ liveth in me." A true believer, a true Christian, is conformed by the renewing of his mind into the image of Christ, into the life of Christ, into the mind of Christ, into the graces of Christ. He is more and more changed into Christ, so that, in a sense, he may be called Christ, as the Church is in 1 Corinthians 12:12. The Church is called Christ because the Church is transformed into the image of Christ. So every true, believing soul is transformed more and more into Christ daily. 2 Corinthians 3:18: "But we all, with open face, beholding as in a glass the glory of the Lord," that is, of the Lord Jesus, "are changed into the same image, from

glory to glory, even as by the Spirit of the Lord."

Now, then, beloved, reflect upon yourselves and deal impartially with your own souls. If you find these things, there's an abundance of comfort for you, and you will have an abundance of peace when you come to die. And if it is not so with you, labor to have it so; do not suffer Satan, or the flesh, or anything else to delude and deceive you in a business of such great concern. Christ said, "If any thirsts, let him come; come to Me."

The last use is one of exhortation. Seeing that the Lord Christ invites us to come to Him, let us say, "Why, Lord, dost Thou say, 'Come'? Then here I am, here I am. I come, Lord, I come. With my whole heart I desire it. I am sorry I have stayed so long from Thee. I come, O Lord. I come, I come!" How would this delight the Lord to see such a frame of spirit in a congregation, that sinners would come unto Him! You have heard how desirous Christ is of it, and why He is so desirous. Well, let us come to the Lord Jesus. And here let me propound some things to promote this exhortation:

1. Consider our own condition, what we are outside of Christ, what we are without Christ; are we not all men of blood? You read in the law of cities of refuge, and that when a manslayer was pursued by the avenger, unless he got to the city of refuge, he was a dead man. Why, all the men in the world are in that state: they are all murderers. We, by sinning in Adam, fell from God and have murdered our own souls. We are pursued by the devil, and there's no city of refuge but Christ. That's the meaning of it. The cities of refuge were a type of Christ; and as these men, flying to the cities of refuge, were preserved alive, so poor sinners flying to Christ shall be preserved from Satan, who seeks to

murder us all for eternity.

Therefore consider what you are without Christ. We are men who are sick, sick unto death; and there's no physician who can heal us but Christ. We are men who have leprosy, and it cleaves so to us that it will be our death unless we have the blood of Christ to cleanse this leprosy. We are blind, and unless we have a guide we shall fall into the ditch, the ditch of hell, out of which there is no recovery. Therefore come to Christ. He is a Guide who will guide you in the way everlasting. He will lead us so that we shall never fall into the ditch. Oh, come unto Christ. We are all under the law; we are accursed creatures. The law says that every man or woman who does not fulfill all things in the law is cursed. Cursed is everyone who thinks but a vain thought, who speaks but an idle word; cursed is every man who has done amiss, who has deceived his neighbor, and the like.

Now, who must take off the curse? None but Christ, who was made a curse by hanging upon the tree. Oh, therefore, come to Christ; choose Christ; close with Christ; venture your souls upon Jesus Christ; trust in Him and Him alone; resign yourselves up wholly to Him.

Consider what you shall have by coming to Christ. Who is able to tell you that? If a man had the tongue of men and angels he could not set out what poor sinners shall have by Christ.

You shall have pardon of all your sins. You shall have peace of conscience that passes understanding. You shall have sound illumination, and know God and Christ, which is life eternal. You shall have Christ's wisdom, Christ's righteousness, Christ's sanctification,

Christ to be your redemption. You shall have the hidden manna; you shall have the white stone; you shall have the new name; you shall be made a pillar in the temple of God; you shall be made a member of Christ; you shall be made a temple of the Holy Spirit; you shall have the indwelling of the Father, the Son, and the Spirit everlastingly in your souls. Would you have everything that heaven has, that God has, that Christ has? Come to Christ and you shall have it.

Consider who it is who invites you to Christ. It is not Moses; it is not Abraham; it is not Ahasuerus; it is not Esther, but a greater one than any of these, a greater one than all of these. When Moses spoke to Pharaoh, he prevailed with him to let the people go to Mount Sinai. Abraham and Lot prevailed with angels to come in and eat with them. Ahasuerus prevailed with the nobles of 127 provinces to come and feast with him. Esther prevailed with Ahasuerus to show mercy to Mordecai and the Jews, and to destroy Haman. Shall these prevail, and shall not the Lord Jesus Christ prevail, who is greater than all these?

Christ was greater than Moses. Moses was a servant, but Christ was a Son in the house. Abraham rejoiced to see the day of Christ, and he saw it. Ahasuerus was but an earthly prince, but Christ is the prince of life, the prince of all the kings of the earth, an eternal prince. Esther was a poor captive, and Christ is the Master of the marriage feast. Shall the Lord Christ now entreat, invite, and beseech you to come in to Him, and will you not hearken? Pharaoh hearkened to Moses; will you not hearken to Christ? Angels hearkened to Abraham and Lot; will you not hearken to Christ? Nobles hearkened to Ahasuerus; will you not hearken to Christ?

Ahasuerus hearkened to Esther, and will you not hearken to Christ? "Let him that is athirst come," said Christ. "It is I who speaks to you, who is the Son of God, who is the Savior of the world, who is the everlasting Father, who is the Lord of Glory, who has heaven at My disposal." Come, come, oh, come in then to the Lord Jesus! Let not your sins, let not devils, let not the world or lusts keep you back from the Lord Jesus!

And what is it that Christ calls you for? Why does He invite you? Is it for your hurt? Is it to upbraid you for your sin? Is it to check you for your infirmities? Is it to revile and reproach you for any miscarriages? If it were so, then you might demur; then you might argue the case; then you might give a denial. But it is for none of these; it is for your good, and wholly for your good. God and Christ have no designs upon men, as here men have designs upon one another. If they invite you to a feast, many times they have a design on you; but God and Christ have no such designs upon you. It is purely, merely, and totally for your good. The Lord invites you so that you may partake of His righteousness; so that you may have His wisdom, His Spirit, His fullness, His grace, His glory; so that you may be happy as He is happy. Christ gets nothing by it; you have all the gain and all the benefit.

Consider that Christ's tendering Himself unto you is the greatest mercy that heaven has to offer unto poor sinners. What has God in heaven now to do your poor souls good with besides Christ? The Spirit does not come unless Christ sends Him. The Father has promised Him the sending of the Spirit, but God holds out Christ to you: "God so loved the world that He gave His only begotten Son." It is the greatest mercy, I say, that heaven has to offer you. And this day, in the name of the great God, I offer Jesus Christ unto you all. Come in and receive Christ; receive the Lord Jesus Christ to be your Husband, to be your King, to be your Prophet, to be your high Priest, to be your Savior, to be all in all to you. And know that if you refuse and will not receive Christ now offered to you; if you will not let go of your lusts, drunkenness, whoredom, envy, malice, slandering, and the like; if you will not let go of these for Christ, your damnation will be upon your own heads. Salvation is brought to your doors. Christ is laid before you. He is held out to you. The golden scepter this day is held out unto you. Oh, receive the Lord Jesus Christ!

And if you do not, know that you provoke God more in refusing Christ than by all the sins that you ever committed. This is the sin that will be your damnation. John 3:19: "This is the condemnation, that light is come into the world, and men love darkness rather than light." They love darkness; they love sin, sinful ways, sinful lusts, sinful company, and sinful practices. If you love these, this is the condemnation: when men will not receive Christ, they make God a liar. And what an injury this is to God, that you will put the lie upon God, as if God did *not* love the world, as if God did *not* hold out Christ to save sinners. And if you receive Him not, you do not bear witness to the truth of God and set your seal that God is true, and so thereby honor Him. Therefore be persuaded to come in and honor the Lord Jesus. What will make it so hard with those of Capernaum and Jerusalem at the last day is that Christ was their Prophet, and was offered unto them, but they would have none of Him. "We will not have this man to rule over us. This is the heir; come, let us kill Him."

Therefore it shall be easier for Sodom and Gomorrah at the day of judgment; it shall be easier for Constantinople at the day of judgment than for Stepney [the city in which Greenhill ministered], for those of you who will not leave your sinful courses and fall in with Christ, and live for Christ, and look for glory hereafter.

Why, you shall not always be here. Soon will come your eternal condition, and why will you lose eternity for momentary pleasure and momentary riches? Why will you lose glory, lose all, and have that which will aggravate your misery a thousand times more? Had you not lived where the gospel is preached, when you come to die it would not have been so bad; but when you might have had Christ, and might have had salvation and heaven, and you have neglected this, it will trouble you and lie sad upon you to all eternity—and this will sink you deeper into hell. There, mercy will be your torment; mercy will be your hell; mercy will be your damnation. And so it will prove to be for all eternity to all who live under the means and do not come to Christ.

Suppose that a man is in a rotten boat at sea. There is a great storm rising and many pirates abroad. And the admiral of the sea, seeing his condition, sends to him, saying, "Friend, friend, come in to me and I will secure you." But the man refuses, and soon he is taken by the pirates, carried away, and put into a dungeon. Now what is it that troubles this man so? The admiral's kindness which he spurned. So it will be with sinners. Christ, the Admiral of the sea, calls to poor sinners, "Come in to Me. I will save you from the storm. I will save soul and body for all eternity." But you refuse, and at last you are taken and cast into hell; and there you lie with this upon your souls: that you might have had mercy and would not. Oh, therefore, come in to Jesus Christ! Stand out no longer, but come and give yourselves up to Him. Live like Christ, and you shall have a heaven here, and a heaven hereafter.

The Water of Life,
Part 1

"And whosoever will, let him take the
water of life freely." Revelation 22:17

This is the last invitation of Christ unto sinners in
the whole Book of God, and as sweet an invitation as
ever sinners met with. "And whosoever will, let him
take the water of life freely."

You have here in these words, first, the thing tendered, "the water of life"; second, the persons to whom
the tender is made, "whosoever will"; third, the manner
of this tender, "freely"; and then the invitation itself:
"let him take." And I will now open these words.

"Whosoever will" means the willing man, the willing one. Christ said in John 5:6 to the man who had
lain long at the pool of Bethesda, "Wilt thou be made
whole?" The man said, "I am very willing to be made
whole, but I cannot get into the pool. I have no might
or power to get into the pool. I am a lame man, and
when the angel stirs the pool one or another gets in
before me, and so I get no benefit."

Christ said to him, "Art thou willing to be healed?"

"Yes," said the man.

"Then I am willing to heal you."

This willingness that Christ requires does not suppose any power of free will in man, but a willingness in
man to receive; for man does not have this willingness
in him naturally. Christ requires a willingness, but this

163

willingness is not in man naturally. Romans 8:7: "The carnal mind is enmity to God; for it is not subject to the law of God, neither indeed can be." 2 Corinthians 3:5: "We are not sufficient of ourselves to think a good thought." There's no willingness in us. Colossians 1:21: "You were enemies to God through wicked works in your minds." If the mind is at enmity with God, there is no willingness to close with God. Philippians 2:13 tells us that both the will and the deed are from God.

Then how does this willingness that Christ requires come? It arises from the promise. When a promise is made freely and generally of some choice and great mercy, the very promise begets a willingness in man. When a prince propounds some great reward if men do such and such a thing, it begets a willingness in them where there was none before. So when God or Christ propounds water of life, salvation, and eternal happiness unto men, and tells them of such a good, and promises it unto them, the very promise begets a willingness in men where it was not before.

"Let him take." With his hands? No, this water of life is not to be taken with your hands; it is to be taken by faith. We are to solicit God by our prayers, and to take His answer by our faith. God does not thrust water of life upon men unwillingly, or upon people who are slothful and sleepy; but He offers water of life to those who are willing and industrious, who seek it. Let those take it.

"Let him take the water of life." What is this water of life? There is a variety of interpretations of these words. Some make this water of life to be Christ, the Fountain of living water, the Fountain of grace and glory. Some make this water to be the Spirit, who is called "water" frequently in Scripture. Some make this water to be the doctrine of the gospel. Some make this water to be grace. And I think none of these are out of the question, but all may be taken in. Christ is water of life; the Spirit is water of life; the doctrine of the gospel, or the gospel itself, is water of life; the gifts and graces of the Spirit are water of life.

And why are they likened to water? I might spend much time here in showing you the resemblances, but I will only name them.

1. Water cleanses from filth and pollution, and so does the Word of God; so does the gospel; so does grace; so does the Spirit; so does Christ. "You are clean through the word that I have spoken," said Christ in John 15:3.

2. Water softens and mollifies the hard earth; so do the doctrine of the gospel, that heavenly dew, the graces of the Spirit, the Spirit itself, and Christ Himself, soften the heart where they come. Paul was a sour piece, a stubborn, hard-hearted sinner; but when he met with Christ, and some of this water fell upon his heart, he said, "What wilt Thou have me to do, Lord?" He was soft, mollified, and melted.

3. Water is of a cooling nature: it cools the heat of the air and the heat of the earth. So this water of life cools the heat of temptation, the heat of persecution, the heat of your lusts, the heat of anger and passion. Where any of this water comes, it cools your unnatural heat, and those sinful heats which we have contracted.

4. Water makes the earth fruitful. So where any of this water of life comes, it makes men and women fruitful. When Christ said to Zacchaeus, "This day is salvation come to thy house," how fruitful was he immedi-

ately: "The half of my goods I give to the poor." The water of the gospel and the Spirit makes men and women wonderfully fruitful.

5. Water satisfies thirst. This water of life is the only water that satisfies thirsty souls. When you have a promise given, and when Christ and the Spirit come in, and when divine truths are let into your hearts, how are you satisfied and refreshed!

6. Water cures and heals diseases and distempers of the body. You go to the waters, to the wells, to the baths, and use other waters which are healing waters. The waters of the gospel are healing waters. Christ sent out His Word and healed people. Christ said to the leper, "I will; be thou clean." And he was clean. The Word of God will heal all diseases of your souls. It is not only a pattern of wholesome words, but a pattern of healing words.

7. Some waters are very comfortable and cordial. So are these waters of life. Is not this text very cordial to think upon? "Whosoever will, let him come and take of the water of life freely."

QUESTION. Upon what accounts is it called "the water of life"?

ANSWER. First of all, this water begets life. Take Christ Himself for the water of life, for Christ Himself is life. He is both the Prince of life, and He is life itself. John 14:6: "I am the life." Colossians 3:3: "When Christ, who is our life, shall appear, we shall appear with Him in glory." Christ brought life to a dead world; He is water of life.

Take the Spirit for water of life. The Spirit begets life in the soul. It is a Spirit of life, and it is called living water. John 7:38: "He that believeth on Me (as the Scripture hath said), out of his belly shall flow rivers of living water." And this He spoke of the Spirit. The Spirit is water of life unto men and women.

Take it for the gospel. Philippians 2:16 says that it is the word of life. The very Word begets life in men and women. 1 Peter 1:23: "Being born not of corruptible seed, but of incorruptible, by the living and abiding Word of God." The Word of God lives and begets life in men and women. It is seed, and all true seed has life in it. Sow any corn, and it has life in it. This is divine and heavenly corn, and when it is sown in your hearts it begets life there.

Grace is life; faith is life; all grace is life. It is the life of the soul, so that these things are called waters of life because these waters beget life.

Second, they are waters of life because they maintain life. We are nourished by the same things of which we consist, says the philosopher. And the theologian similarly says that we consist of divine principles; a godly man is made up of the Word of God, the divine nature, and the graces of the Spirit. And we are maintained by the same: by Christ, by the Spirit, by the Word, and by this water of life. We live upon the same. Therefore Christ, grace, and the Spirit are compared in Scripture to things upon which men live. Isaiah 55:1: "Ho, everyone that thirsteth." It is by things like water, wine, milk, marrow, and bread that men live. Isaiah 55:3: "Incline your ear and come unto Me; hear and your souls shall live." Your life shall be maintained by these things. Christ is the bread of life and the water of life, and we must live by this bread and water: by the flesh of Christ, by the blood of Christ, by the promises of Christ, by the graces of Christ, and by the Spirit of Christ. These maintain life in men and women.

Third, it's water of life because it makes us more and more lively. It not only begets and maintains life, but it increases life, and it makes us lively. John 4:14 says that this water shall be a well of water springing up into everlasting life. It increases life, and springs up into more and more life. Christ says in John 10:10, "I am come that ye might have life, and have it in more abundance." How lively was Peter after the water of the Spirit came upon him in Acts 2! And it is this Peter who writes of living and lively stones. Christians should not only be living but lively; and this water makes us lively, full of the Spirit.

Fourth, and last, it is water of life because it brings us unto everlasting life. He who has the gospel comes to be a partaker of the Spirit; and he who has the Spirit is a partaker of Christ; and he who is a partaker of Christ comes to God. See how this water of life springs up into everlasting life. Christ says in John 14:6, "I am the way, the truth, and the life. No man cometh unto the Father but by Me." By Christ we come to the Father.

Romans 8:9: "He that hath not the Spirit is none of Christ's." And he who does not have the gospel does not have the ministration of the Spirit where the gospel waters come. This water is conveyed to the soul. There the Spirit is, and there Christ is, and there's coming to the Father. Thus it springs up from the gospel to the Spirit, from the Spirit to Christ, and from Christ to the Father, as in John 4:14. It is a well springing up into everlasting life. This water came from the Father, and it will carry men up to the Father into everlasting life. So, then, you see what this water of life is, and why it is said to be water of life.

How are we to take this water? "Let him take of the water of life freely." There's something in this word "freely." It notes, first, that, let a sinner be what he will, there is no bar put in against him to keep him off from this water. Let a man be a great sinner, an old sinner, let his sins be crimson and scarlet sins, God puts in no bar. Christ does not say, "Let a little sinner," or "a young sinner," or "a sinner who has sinned once or twice, or a hundred or a thousand times," come, but He says, "Let whosoever will come; let him take of the water of life freely. Let his sins be what they will, all manner of blasphemies shall be forgiven." There's no bar except against the unpardonable sin; but whatever sin, though long continued in, though of the most heinous nature, though clothed with the most dreadful aggravations, yet it shall be forgiven. Let that sinner come and take of this water of life freely. A man who is leprous all over may as freely go into the river or sea and wash himself as the man who is sound. There is no bar in his way.

Second, it imports that whatever qualifications men have—let them be honest, moral, civil, sober, righteous, just, with good natures and dispositions—yet no man deserves or merits anything, not one drop of this water. Many think (and it is the popish doctrine) that men may be made fit for this water, that men deserve this water and are worthy of it. No, let men be never so righteous, never so just or moral, never so civil, yet when they have done all that ever they can, they do not deserve one drop of this water. But whosoever will, let him come and take it freely. There's no merit of yours; there's no deserving; there's no fitness in you, but it is water that is freely prepared and freely given.

Third, it imports that men may come and take abundantly of this water. When you invite persons into your orchard, gardens, wine cellars, you say, "Come, eat and drink what you will." And that expresses the freedom you give them, that they may take abundantly. So here, whosoever will, let him come and take freely; let him eat; let him drink; let him satisfy himself. There is no measure set that you shall have so much and no more. You may have a pint, a quart, a bottle, or a vessel full. There are no limits set, but take as much as you will, as much as you can carry away (John 10:10; James 1:5).

Fourth, and last, it imports that whatever endeavors men use, let men strive and endeavor never so much, yet it is not because of their endeavors that they shall have this water. Men must strive; they must read, hear, and pray; they must dig for wisdom as for silver and gold. But when they have done all, it is God who gives this water. God gives it, but He gives it in the use of the means—*in* their digging, *in* their laboring, *in* their waiting, but not *for* their digging, not *for* their laboring, not *for* their waiting. Romans 9:16: "It is not in him that willeth, or in him that runneth, but in God that showeth mercy." It is water freely given.

Thus you have the words opened, and now I shall come to the point I shall insist upon.

DOCTRINE: The offer of the water of life is free.

"Whosoever will, let him take the water of life freely." It is freely offered unto men. Take Christ for the water of life; He is freely offered unto the world. John 3:16: "For God so loved the world that He gave His only begotten Son, that whosoever believeth in Him should not perish." What is freer than a gift? God has given

Him; therefore Christ said in John 4:10 to the woman of Samaria, "If thou knewest the gift of God, and who it is that saith unto thee, "Give Me to drink,' thou wouldest have asked of Him, and He would have given thee water of life." Christ is the gift of God. He is freely given, freely offered unto the sons of men. Romans 8:32: "He that spared not His own Son, but delivered Him up for us all." God did not spare Him, but freely delivered Him up for us all. So this water of life is freely tendered and given unto you.

The Spirit is freely tendered unto men. Ezekiel 36:25, 27: "I will sprinkle clean water upon them, and wash them from all their filthiness. I will put My Spirit into them." Joel 2:28: "I will pour out My Spirit upon all flesh." The Lord tenders this water of life freely. Christ says in Luke 11:13: "If ye that are evil can give good gifts unto your children, how much more shall My Father give the Spirit to them that ask Him?"

The gospel is freely given. Christ said to His disciples, "Freely ye have received, freely give." And in Mark 16:15: "Go preach the gospel to every creature." The gospel is the ministration of grace, the ministration of the Spirit. All the water of life is freely given. Revelation 21:6: "And He said unto me, 'It is done. I am Alpha and Omega, the beginning and the end. I will give unto him that is athirst of the fountain of the water of life freely.' " Christ will give freely.

And as this water of life is freely given, so it is freely revealed. God made it known freely. Matthew 13:11: "To you it is given to know." No one else made it known. God might have kept this fountain shut up in heaven and never revealed it, never made known to the world any such water, any such grace, any such mercy as is here held out to you. Hence it is that Christ said to Peter in Matthew 16:17, after Peter had made his confession regarding Christ being the Son of the living God, "Blessed art thou, Simon Barjona, for flesh and blood hath not revealed this unto thee." God had revealed it unto him. And Matthew 11:25: "I thank Thee, O Father, Lord of heaven and earth, that Thou hast hidden these things from the wise and prudent, and hast revealed them unto babes." God reveals this water and makes it known.

And as God reveals it, so it is the Lord who blesses this water, and makes it a blessing to one and not unto another. This water was a blessing unto Peter; it was not a blessing unto Judas. Judas had no blessing by the gospel, no blessing by Christ. Those of Capernaum had no blessing. It is God who gives the water, reveals the water, and blesses this water to whomever He pleases.

QUESTION. Why does the Lord freely offer and tender this water of life unto the world, unto sinners?

ANSWER. This water of life is freely offered, first, so that God might make known His goodness and make way for His glory. Things that come freely reveal the goodness of the person who gave them, and redound most to their praise and honor. When a parent, out of his own generosity, gives a child great matters, unlooked for, unsought for, unthought of, this argues the goodness of the parent and draws more honor. When a prince shall bestow gifts upon his subjects out of his own bounty and good will, not moved by his nobles, princes, or others around him, this declares his goodness and makes way for his honor, and everyone says, "What a good prince this is," or "What a good king this is." And how honorable is this when he does it freely and no one has moved him to do it!

When men are moved to do good, those who move them share in the good; they share in the honor, for had not the party been so moved, it would not have been done. Now God will have none to share in His honor. God does it freely, according to the counsel of His own will, for His own name, so that His goodness may be known and His honor may be great. "Be it known unto you," said God in Ezekiel 36:22, "that not for your sakes do I this, but for My own name's sake." It is as if He had said, "I do it not because you move Me, or because anyone else moves Me, but I do it from within, for My own will." And so His goodness appears, and His honor is greater.

Second, the Lord tenders water of life freely so that He may take away all objections, all scruples and fears which usually lie in the hearts of sinners. When people have sinned against God, when they are guilty and unholy, they are afraid of God. Adam ran from God and hid himself. People have hard thoughts of God, and think that God will not be pacified towards them. To prevent this, the Lord takes away all such objections, scruples, and fears out of the minds of men and women, and freely offers water of life. He freely holds out the golden scepter, freely offers pardon, peace, grace, and salvation.

Third, the Lord does this so that He may endear our hearts the more unto Him. When a thing comes freely from others, how it takes hold of the heart; it knits the heart much unto that person. In 2 Samuel 7, the Lord comes to David and tells him what great matters He would do for him and his house. Then in verses 18–19: "Then went King David and sat before the Lord and said, 'Who am I, O Lord God, and what is my father's house, that Thou hast brought me hitherto? And this was yet a small thing in Thy sight, O Lord God. But Thou hast also spoken of Thy servant's house for a great while to come, and is this the manner of men, O Lord God?' " What, will God deal thus by man, to come to him and offer him such kindness and such mercy, to deal so bountifully and freely with him? Is this the manner of men? This is the manner of God to deal with man so that He may endear their hearts unto Him. When things are done freely and unexpectedly, they endear and engage the heart abundantly.

Fourth, and last, the Lord freely holds out grace and mercy to sinners to prevent pride and boasting. Were there any free will, power, or qualification in man which might move or draw God to bestow and give these waters, man would be ready to attribute the thing to himself, and to glory and boast. Now, that man may not glory or boast, the Lord freely bestows and gives the water of life. 1 Corinthians 1:27–29: "God hath chosen the foolish things of the world to confound the wise, and hath chosen the weak things of the world to confound the things which are mighty. The base things of the world, and things which are despised, yea, hath He chosen, and things which are not, to bring to nought the things which are, that no flesh should glory in His presence." God would have none glory in His presence; therefore He takes things that are most unlikely, foolish, weak, contemptible, and despised.

Application

1. Does the Lord freely offer water of life unto us? Then this serves to reprove those who refuse to receive this water.

But, you will say, are there any such in the world? What, will any refuse such water of life? Can there be any such person living?

Yes, beloved, too many. The world is full of them; it always was, and now is full of such. And that I may not give you words only, take Scripture. Psalm 81:11: "But My people would not hearken to My voice, and Israel would have none of Me." Mark it, "My people," said God, "would not hearken to My voice." It is as if He had said, "I came and told them of water, and water of life. I set life and death before them, but My people would not hearken to My voice. They would have none of Me, the Fountain of living waters." Though God was the Fountain of living waters, they would have none of Him. Israel itself would have none of Him. And Isaiah 65:2: "I have spread out My hands all the day unto a rebellious people, which walketh in a way which is not good, after their own thoughts." God is saying, "I have all the day spread out My hands to them, held out water of life unto them, and they would have none of Me." Proverbs 1:24–25: "I have called and ye refused. I have stretched out My hands, and no man regarded, but set at naught all My counsels, and would have none of My reproof." It was quite frequent in those days for men to have none of the water of life.

And was it not so in Christ's time, and the time of the apostles? Matthew 23:37: "O Jerusalem, Jerusalem, how often would I have gathered thee, as a hen doth her chickens, and ye would not." Christ would have had them receive water of life, but they would not. John 1:11 tells us that "He came unto His own, and His own received Him not." Acts 13:46: "It was necessary that the gospel should first have been preached unto you, but seeing ye put it from you we turn to the Gentiles." So it is in all ages: the greatest part of people refuse the water of life and choose strange waters instead (2 Kings 19:24; Hebrews 3:13). They follow strange doctrines, strange opinions, strange blasphemies, puddle waters, and poisoned waters; but as for the waters of life, they will have none of them.

Now see the evil in refusing these waters of life. This will appear, first, if you consider what it is that they refuse: it is water of life. If it were ill, bitter, corrupt, or poisoned water, it would be something; but it's water of life, water that begets life, maintains life, increases life, and brings unto life everlasting. The more excellent any thing is that is refused, the greater is the evil in refusing it. To refuse a bag of dust, to refuse a bottle of some musty liquor would be nothing; but to refuse a wedge of gold or a bottle of fine spirits shows folly and weakness. Who in his right mind would refuse God when He is offered, water of life when it is offered? It is the most excellent thing, and yet men refuse it.

Second, it is that which is freely offered. If it were offered upon hard terms, if men were to buy it at a dear cost, if they had to bring bags of money for it, there would be some reason to refuse it. Not everyone has bags of money, as Simon Magus had. But it's not to be sold for money; it's freely given, and when a commodity of such infinite worth is offered freely to you and you will have none of it, your sin is great. It was freely offered, and you would have none of it.

Third, consider who offers it. It is offered by Christ, by the ministers of Christ. It is offered to you daily by Christ. Now shall Christ, who is the Son of God, the Prince of life, the Heir of the world, who is worshipped by angels, who is the great Commander of heaven and earth, come and offer you water of life, and yet you will have none of it? Shall He who loves sinners and laid down His life for them, who would wash them in His blood, come and tender the gospel and grace to you, and will you have none thereof? Your sin is great, exceedingly great.

Fourth, consider that it is the greatest ingratitude that ever was in men and women that Christ should bring water of life, and freely offer it to you, which you have extreme need of, and yet you will have none of it. He does it out of love, aiming at your good and the saving of your souls; and yet you will have none of this water. What ingratitude is this! Christ may say, "I brought water to your door, and such water as was water of life. It would have quickened you, maintained life in you, and brought you to eternal life; and you would have none of it." Hear, O heavens, and hearken, O earth; was there ever such ingratitude?

Fifth, consider that this water of life is the only remedy that can do your souls good. It's the mercy of God in Christ; it's Christ's merits. The Spirit, and the graces thereof, must do sinners good if anything in heaven and earth can do them good. There is nothing in heaven and earth besides free grace and mercy, this water of life, which can do your souls good. If you will not drink of this water, you must die. You must die and perish forever. Jonah said of the people, "They embrace lying vanities, and forsake their own mercies" (Jonah 2:8). So all men and women in the world embrace lying vanities who forsake these waters. They will drink the muddy waters of the world, the filthy waters of sin, the ditches of Rome, the puddles of Egypt and Babylon; but of these waters which would save their souls, they will not drink. This is an evil against the remedy.

Sixth, consider that the refusal of these waters provokes God and Christ greatly to wrath. You cannot provoke God more than by refusing His kindness. You grieve, you vex the Spirit; you resist the Spirit and so provoke God bitterly. Psalm 81:11–12: "My people would not hearken to My voice, and Israel would have none of Me; so I gave them up to their own hearts' lusts." It is as if God were saying, "I will scourge them no more, but give them over to the saddest judgments in the world. They shall be left to their own lusts, their own wills and humors. I will leave them now to drink waters that will poison them, waters that will ripen them for hell."

In Luke 14, those who were invited to the supper made excuses, every one of them, and would not come. So Christ said, "Not one of them shall taste of My supper" (verse 24). The meaning is, "They shall not only not taste of the dainties I have prepared, but they shall taste the severity of My wrath. Instead of cups of wine, they shall have cups of brimstone and fire. The vengeance that is written they shall have executed upon them."

When God offered Canaan to the Jews, and they refused it and would instead go back to Egypt, God was so moved that He swore in His wrath, "If they shall not enter into My rest, let them be thrust out of heaven." And the fierceness of God's anger never came upon the Jews till they had refused Christ and these waters of life. But then the wrath of God came upon them to the uttermost; to its fullness it came upon them.

Seventh, and last, regarding those who refuse the waters of life, the Lord Christ and God keep account of all such passages, and will bring them in against them, and urge them as aggravations of their misery at last. The Lord keeps accounts. "I have stretched out My hand all day long," says God. "A whole day, the day of their lives I waited upon them." Revelation 3:20: "Behold, I stand at the door and knock." Christ keeps account of how long He stood there, how many knocks He has made there. How many tenders of grace have been presented to you? How often have you refused and turned them away? He will come at last and say, "At such a place I stood and knocked twenty or thirty years. And in such a place I tendered grace to them a thousand times, and My Spirit presented good motions to them ten thousand times; yet they refused."

All these will be brought in at last, and then when you see this black bill, this will sink you into the bottom of hell. Grace offered, peace offered, heaven offered, Christ and His righteousness offered—all were offered to be your portion; and you would have none of them. And what did you choose instead? Chaff, earth, puddle water? Your misery will be exceedingly great.

The Water of Life, Part 2

"And whosoever will, let him take the water of life freely." Revelation 22:17

We come now to a use of exhortation. If the waters of life are freely offered, then here's an invitation to all sinners to come and accept these waters. Come, you sinners, whoever you are—you who are in the chambers of death, you who are in the broad way, you who are enemies to God through wicked works in your mind, you who have lived basely to the dishonor of God and man and to your own prejudice and damnation. If you will come, here are waters of life, waters that will give life to the dead. Here are waters to increase life; here are waters to be had freely. Come to these waters; they are held forth upon such terms that you may all come and receive them. "Whosoever will, let him come and take of the water of life." Isaiah 55:7: "Let the wicked forsake his ways, and the unrighteous his thoughts, and turn unto the Lord, and He shall have mercy."

Proverbs 28:13: "He that confesses his sins and forsakes them shall find mercy." There the terms are somewhat hard. Who can forsake his ways and turn from his evil thoughts? It's a hard thing to do, but here it is upon these terms: "Whosoever will, let him come and take of the waters of life freely." You may have them freely. Whatsoever your sins have been—crimson sins, scarlet sins, crying sins, sins against light or nature,

180

against law, against heaven, against earth, sins against the state, against the Church, against body or soul, sins against the gospel—whatever your sins have been, here are waters of life freely for you.

Abraham was an idolater, and yet he had water of life freely. Saul was a persecutor, and he had water of life freely. And why may you not have waters of life freely? A man may go and take water at any well in town; he may go to the Thames and take what water he will. When the rain falls, who may not have a share of it? Here's water, here's rain from heaven; and whoever will may come and take this water of life.

Sometimes money is given in a place for poor people, and it is made known for them to come and fetch it; but first they must get petitions, justices, ministers, and others to testify of their honesty, of their faithfulness, of their service, of their sufferings, of their losses. There is a great deal for them to do before they can have the money. But it is not so here. Christ does not say, "Let him who is righteous come; let him who is so qualified take it; let him who has suffered such hard things, let him who has been tempted so long by Satan come." No, He says, "Whosoever will, let him take the waters of life freely."

What, will you stand out then and not receive waters of life? Oh, come in this day! Come to Christ; come in and drink the waters of life; come in and live; come and live comfortably; come and live eternally.

If the water of life is freely offered to sinners, then you who are barren and dead-hearted, who complain of unfruitfulness and unprofitableness, wait upon the Lord Christ in the use of means; for here is water of life, and Christ gives it out in the use of means. Are you dry, barren, and fruitless? Have you a dead heart? Christ has water of life to quicken you. Christ has water of life to make you more lively. "I am come," said Christ in John 10:10, "that ye might have life, and that ye might have it in more abundance." Christ is saying, "I have come for the very purpose of giving life, and to give life more abundantly, to give out these waters freely and fully." When the rain falls from heaven upon the mountains and barren places, it will make them look green. So when Christ gives out these waters to mountainous hearts, to barren spirits, this water of life will soak into you, soften you, make you grow and flourish, and bring forth fruit.

Lamentations 3:25: "The Lord is good unto them that wait for Him, to the soul that seeketh Him." It is good that a man should both hope and quietly wait for the salvation of the Lord. "The Lord is good to them that wait for Him." If you will wait for Christ in His ordinances, he will be good unto you. He will water you and make you a watered garden. Isaiah 40:28–29, 31: "Hast thou not known, hast thou not heard, that the everlasting God, the Lord, the Creator of the ends of the earth fainteth not, neither is weary? There is no searching of His understanding. He giveth power to the faint, and to them that have no might He increaseth strength. They that wait upon the Lord shall renew their strength; they shall mount up with wings as eagles; they shall run and not be weary, and they shall walk and not faint." Wait upon the Lord Christ. He has virtue for you. He has waters of life for you.

Isaiah 64:4–5: "For since the beginning of the world, men have not heard, nor perceived by the ear, neither hath the eye seen, O God, besides Thee, what He hath prepared for him that waiteth for Him. Thou meetest him that rejoiceth and worketh righteousness." Those who remember God in His ways, He will meet them. He will water and refresh them, and they shall be fruitful. You made the Lord Christ wait for your tears. He waited a long time before you shed one tear of repentance, and will you not wait upon Him who has water of life for you? Wait upon Him in the use of means, and He will give water of life.

You who have received water of life, remember how little it cost you. Give the honor and glory unto God. It cost you nothing; you had it freely. Psalm 115:1: "Not unto us, O Lord, not unto us, but unto Thy name give glory." Yea, give all the praise and all the glory. If we contributed anything to this work of grace and salvation, then we might sacrifice to our own nets; but we contribute nothing. Ephesians 2:8–9: "By grace are ye saved through faith, and that not of yourselves. *It is the gift of God, not of works,* lest any man should boast."

The Lord knew what man would do if he should come in and be a co-worker with God. Therefore He said, "By grace are ye saved through faith, and that not of yourselves. It is the gift of God." If you have faith, if you have grace, if you have salvation, water of life, it is the gift of God, not of works, lest any man should boast. Therefore, let no man glory in himself, but give the honor and glory to God. Jeremiah 9:23–24: "Let not the wise man glory in his wisdom, neither let the mighty man glory in his might, let not the rich man glory in his riches; but let him that glorieth glory in this, that he understandeth and knoweth Me, that I am the Lord which exerciseth loving-kindness." Isaiah 43:25: "I, even I am He that blotteth out thy transgressions for Mine own sake, and will not remember thy sins." He does not do it for our sake, but for His own sake. For the honor of His own name He blots out our sins, He pardons us, and gives us water of life.

So, then, let us give God the honor and the glory, and say as it is in Micah 7:18: "Who is a God like unto Thee, that pardoneth iniquity, and passeth by the transgression of the remnant of His heritage? He retaineth not His anger forever, because He delights in mercy." Who is a God like unto our God, who pardons iniquities, sins, and transgressions? And why? Because He delights in mercy; not because He delights in you or me, but because He delights in mercy. He delights to show mercy. He blots out sins freely for the honor of His own name. Therefore you have pardon of sin and peace of conscience. If you have any grace, any comfort of the Spirit—if you have any drops of this water of life—give God the glory of it. He has freely given it unto you, and that in abundance, when others have none, or only puddle water.

If God gives us water of life freely, then this should unite and endear our hearts to Him, and make us serve Him freely. As He freely gives to us, so we should freely serve Him. Many reluctantly serve God; the Sabbaths are tedious to them, and they are anxious for them to be over. Prayer, reading Scripture, hearing sermons, and discoursing of heavenly things are all tedious to them; they cannot endure them. It's an argument that they are fleshly and corrupt, that they have none of this water of life. If they did, they would serve God freely, cheerfully, and willingly. Philippians 2:13–14: "It is God that worketh in you both to will and to do of His own good pleasure. Do all things without murmuring or

disputing." When God works in men, according to His
good pleasure, the will and the deed, then men will do
all things without murmuring and disputing. They will
come off roundly and readily to do the work of God.
They will then be like David, who fulfilled all the will of
God, and gave this counsel to his son in 1 Chronicles
28:9: "And thou, Solomon, my son, know thou the God
of thy father, and serve Him with a perfect heart, and
with a willing mind." God does not regard any of your
services that come off heavily, dully, and with murmuring; but God loves a cheerful giver, a willing mind. He
is free Himself, and gives water of life freely, and He
would have you serve Him cheerfully and willingly.

But to proceed to another observation: "Whosoever
will, let him take the waters of life freely." Whosoever
will is literally "the willing man."

The first observation is this: That man who is willing, or has a willingness to have the waters of life, shall
have them.

Be the man what he will, high or low, rich or poor,
learned or unlearned, young or old, bond or free,
whosoever has a willingness in him to have the waters
of life shall have them. But let us turn to the Scriptures
for proof of this.

John 5:40: "Ye will not come to Me that ye might
have life." It is as if Christ were saying, "You will not
come to Me that you might have waters of life. Were
there in you a willingness to have the waters of life, you
would have them." Isaiah 55:1–2: "Ho, every one that
thirsteth, come ye to the waters; and ye that have no
money, come, buy and eat, yea, come, buy wine and
milk without money and without price." God is saying,
"Are you willing to have waters of life? Are you willing

to have wine and milk without money? You say you have
no money. Will you have them without money? Are you
willing to have them? If you are but willing, you shall
have them. Are you thirsty? You shall have water. I do
not look at your money. I do not look at any qualifications, dispositions, or reparations. I look at this: are you
willing to have it? Why do you spend your money for
that which is not bread, and your labor for that which
satisfies not?"

And because men will not come to Christ, Christ
comes to them. Revelation 3:20: "Behold, I stand at the
door and knock. If any man hear My voice and open
the door, I will come in to him, and will sup with him
and he with Me." Christ comes and stands at the door
and knocks. When someone comes to the door of a
house and knocks, if there is someone inside and they
will not open the door, you cannot come in; but if the
party will open the door, you come in immediately.
Christ comes and knocks now, and He would fain come
in; but men and women will not open the door. What is
this opening the door? Your hearts are the door, and
opening your hearts is your willingness for Christ to
come in; but men and women keep the door shut, and
so Christ does not enter. They have no willingness in
them. There is a will in all men by nature, but there is
not a willingness. If a man has a hand to receive anything, while he keeps his hand shut he can receive
nothing; but if he will open his hand then he is fit to
receive.

A man who keeps his mouth shut can take in no water, no wine, no food. This is the case with sinners: as
long as they keep their hearts shut, Christ knocks, the
Spirit knocks, the minister knocks, the Word knocks,

and God knocks, but they will not open and so there is no entrance. But willingness is the opening of the heart, and makes way for Christ's entrance. Lydia was hearing, and her heart was opened and Christ came in; the waters of life came in. Isaiah 1:19: "If ye be willing and obedient, ye shall eat the fat of the land." If you are willing, you shall have the blessing. There is a willingness required in sinners to receive grace, to receive mercy, to receive the waters of life.

QUESTION. Wherein lies this willingness that should be in sinners to receive the waters of life, to receive grace and mercy?

ANSWER. It lies in three things:

1. In a high prizing of this water of life. When a man comes to have apprehensions of worth and excellency in it, thereupon he prizes what is so apprehended; for you must know that the operations of the will are according to the apprehensions of the understanding. If a man understands that something is worth a great deal, then his will prizes the good that is in the thing answerably. When men have weak apprehensions of things, they do not prize them much, and value them accordingly. But if men apprehend things strongly, and see a great deal of worth and excellence in them, then they prize them accordingly.

2. The soul hereupon comes to make choice of this good for itself. The will chooses this good so apprehended and so prized. When a man beholds a person who is beautiful, amiable, and suitable unto him, he prizes the person and chooses that person for himself. So the will, upon apprehension of the water of life, and the infinite good to be had thereby, chooses this water of life for itself. And thus David said in Psalm 73:25,

"Whom have I in heaven but Thee. And there is none upon earth that my soul desires beside Thee." David saw such worth in Christ that He chose Christ in heaven, on earth, and none besides Him. Hear what the spouse said in Song of Solomon 5:10: "My beloved" (there's the choice) "is white and ruddy, the chiefest of ten thousand." It is as if the spouse had said, "I know what a one my beloved is. I have such apprehensions of him: He is white and ruddy, the chiefest of ten thousand. He is better than all, and therefore I choose Him. He is my beloved." The will comes to choose and take in the object so apprehended for itself. That is the second thing, the will acting in choosing Christ.

3. The will moves and carries the soul to the enjoying of the thing prized and chosen. When a man has cast his eyes upon a virgin and values her, his heart chooses her. Then he uses all lawful means to enjoy her; his will carries him to the use of means. So it is here. The will moves the soul towards Christ, to close with Christ, to enjoy Christ, and acts both inwardly and outwardly.

It acts inwardly by longings, sighings, desires, and thirstings: "Oh, that I had water of life! Oh, that I had water of the well of Bethlehem! Oh, that I had Christ! Oh, that I had the Spirit! Oh, that I had grace."

And then it acts outwardly. It carries the soul to the use of all means—to reading, to hearing, to meditating, to prayer, to conferring, to all the ordinances, and all the other means—that it may enjoy Christ and meet with Him whom it has chosen. This is the willingness that is required. If you are willing; if you have had such apprehensions and prized the water of life, whoever you are; if you have chosen it; if you are moved and carried out to enjoy it—let that soul take the water of life.

QUESTION. Can a man, by his own abilities, make this choice of Christ, of this water of life?

ANSWER. Men may, by their natural abilities, desire the Word and be carried out after it. Amos 8:11–12: " 'Behold the day is come,' saith the Lord God, 'that I will send a famine in the land, not a famine of bread, nor a thirst for water, but of hearing the Word of the Lord; and they shall wander from sea to sea, and from the north even to the east. They shall run to and fro to seek the word of the Lord, and shall not find it.' " Mark it: When the Word should be taken away, they will have a desire, and there will be a motion in them for it. And yet, it is believed, these are not regenerate and godly, but of the ordinary and common sort of people. The work of reason and natural apprehension of some good in the Word carried them after it. But I conceive that no man can, by natural ability, thus will to choose he Lord Jesus Christ in the manner of which we have spoken.

There are Scriptures that hold this point out strongly. Romans 7:11: "Sin, taking occasion by the commandment, deceived me, and by it slew me." Paul was slain, a dead man; how could he move in such a manner, then, towards Christ? Romans 6:11: "Likewise reckon ye also yourselves to be dead indeed unto sin, but alive unto God through Jesus Christ our Lord." Paul said that he was slain through sin, that he had no life naturally of himself.

1 Corinthians 2:14: "But the natural man receiveth not the things of the Spirit of God, for they are foolishness unto him; neither can he know them, because they are spiritually discerned." Some would make this verse apply to young, weak Christians. But Paul says,

"The natural man receiveth not the things of the Spirit of God." A young Christian, having the Spirit of God, would receive the things of the Spirit of God, and would have some spiritual discerning. But the natural man is destitute of the Spirit, for he says, "We have received not the spirit of the world, but the Spirit which is of God."

The natural man who does not have the Spirit does not receive spiritual things; he does not discern them. And that is the meaning of the word. Look at Jude 19 where you have the same word, but here it is translated "sensual": "Sensual, not having the Spirit." He might interpret it as meaning "natural." Now he who does not have the Spirit cannot discern the things of God; he cannot desire them; he cannot receive them. Therefore Christ said unto Peter, "Blessed art thou, Simon Barjona, for flesh and blood hath not revealed this unto thee." Some boast that they come to this by the power of nature, but God has revealed it by the power of His Spirit. 1 Corinthians 1:21: "For after, in the wisdom of God, the world by wisdom knew not God, it pleased God by the foolishness of preaching to save them that believe." All the wisdom of the world did not bring them up to the knowledge of God. So, then, by man's natural ability he is not able to come to this willingness.

QUESTION. To what end, then, are these waters of life freely offered? If a man does not have this power to will to receive these waters, are they not offered in vain?

ANSWER. To this I answer, first, it is not so, it is not in vain; for where the gospel comes there is so much of the mercy, love, and goodness of God held out, such great, precious, and free promises presented unto men that, being heeded, they beget a willingness in sinners to live. A general virtue and power goes with the gospel to do something in the hearts of men and women which they could not do before. When the lodestone touches the needle, it makes an impression and leaves some virtue upon it. Ezekiel 47:8–9: "Whithersoever the waters of the sanctuary do come, they heal the waters." That is, men and women are like the Dead Sea, corrupt, filthy, stinking, and loathsome in their natural condition, but if the waters of the gospel come, those waters do something there, and they enable men to will, and to will otherwise than they could before. Thus, for us who now live under the gospel, if we heed the gospel, there is so much of the grace, mercy, and love of God's Spirit present with it that, if we heed the gospel, something is wrought in our hearts which may enable us to will to receive these waters of life. And their not doing this is sufficient ground for their condemnation.

Second, the Lord tenders these waters of life unto whosoever will so that those persons might beg God for a will to receive these waters, since He is ready to give them these waters. For when they see waters of life held out in such a way that whosoever will may take of them, the soul may well conclude, "Surely God will give me a will to receive these waters if I beg for them." So, if men and women who now have waters of life held out freely come and beg God for this willingness thus—"Lord, give me a will; give me a will to close with Christ, to prize Christ, to move out after Christ"—God, who will give them the waters, will give them the will (Philippians 2:13; Proverbs 16:1).

Third, and last, this will justify God, and this will be the condemnation to the creature, that here's the gospel offered to men freely; that the gospel, if heeded, will beget a power and will in men; that God, if prayed unto, will give them the will, and yet they neglect all. Men's condemnation will be upon their own heads. Where is God to be blamed?

This being so, let me give you the reasons why the Lord holds out waters of life to those who are willing to receive them. Or, to put it in the form of a question, why is this willingness required at our hands?

1. This willingness is required because otherwise men will not take the waters of life. Let God offer them never so freely or never so long, if men are not willing they will not take them; present what you will to a man who does not have a will for something and he will not take it. So present Christ, the Spirit of God, life eternal, heaven and glory, the great and precious promises, pardon of sin, or what you will; if a man has no will he will not take it. Yet willingness is required for taking such. If a man does not have a mouth, it is in vain to offer him meat; if men have no will, they will not receive (Matthew 23:37; Acts 13:46). Therefore God requires willingness for men to receive the waters of life.

2. This willingness is required so that men may not complain; for if men should be brought to drink waters of life by a compulsory act, they will complain of what follows. Therefore Christ said in Matthew 16:24, "If any man will come after Me, let him deny himself, and take up his cross and follow Me."

"If any man *will* come, if a man has a will to follow Me," said Christ, "let him. He will meet with hard things, and if he is not willing, he will complain that I caused him to follow Me." Men must deny themselves, take up crosses, and endure persecutions and temptations. And if they do not come willingly to God's way, they will complain of it. Now God, to prevent complaining about His ways, requires men to be willing.

3. He requires willingness so that the communion between Christ and the soul may be the sweeter. Where there is willingness on both sides, there will be the sweetest life. If the parties do not consent on both sides, you will find that it will be an ill match. But if there is a willingness and a freeness on both sides, there the communion will be the sweeter. So Christ says, "I freely give, and I would have them freely receive." And so there will be a sweet communion between Christ and the soul. "I am my Beloved's," said the spouse, "and my Beloved is mine." There was mutual agreement between them.

4. Last, this willingness is required so that the wisdom of God in governing His Church and the world might not be questioned; for if God forced men into His service, they would say, "Where's the goodness of God? Where's the wisdom of God? This is tyranny! He is forcing men to serve Him!"

Now God will have none be His servants but those who come freely. Psalm 110:3: "In the day of Thy power Thy people shall be willing." And when He speaks it is, "Compel them to come in." Not by clubs or by laws, but by strong arguments does He tell them what the water of life is, what supper is prepared, how great is the excellence of the provision. That may compel them. No other compulsion does God use but the grace of the Spirit, and divine arguments set upon the heart.

OBJECTION. But this seems contrary to John 6:44, where Christ says, "No man comes to me except the Father draw him." It would seem that this is not voluntary and free.

ANSWER. God does not force a man's will, but He sweetly and lovingly takes away the unwilling part of his will, the corruption of his will. Ezekiel 11:19: "I will give them one heart, and I will put a new spirit within you; and I will take the stony heart out of their flesh, and will give them a heart of flesh." It is as if He had said, "I will take away the stoniness, the hardness, the corruption, the enmity and opposition. I will take all these out of you, and will put a new heart and a new spirit into you." Ezekiel 36:26–27: "A new heart also will I give you, and a new spirit will I put within you. I will take away the stony heart out of your flesh, and I will give you a heart of flesh, and I will put My Spirit within you, and cause you to walk in My statutes, and ye shall keep My judgments and do them." He will cause us to walk in His statutes.

QUESTION. What, will He force His statutes on us against our wills?

ANSWER. No, see what the Church says in Song of Solomon 1:4: "Draw me, O Lord; we will run after Thee." When God comes to draw, the soul runs willingly and freely.

So you see that a willingness is required.

The Water of Life, Part 3

"And whosoever will, let him take the
water of life freely." Revelation 22:17

We proceed to the uses of the point, and so finish
the text.

USE 1. If those who are willing shall have the waters
of life, then here it serves for conviction, and convinces
us that all who think and say they have drunk of these
waters of life have not. Everyone thinks he has grace,
has the Spirit, has Christ and God, and that he shall be
saved; but here is clear evidence to the contrary. For
have you had this willingness in you that is required?
Have men seen such excellence in these waters as to
prize them above all? Have you so prized them as to
choose them above all things in the world? Have you so
chosen them as to pursue getting them to the utmost of
your power? Few have done so.

Matthew 7:21–23: "Not everyone that saith unto Me,
'Lord, Lord,' shall enter into the kingdom of heaven,
but he that doth the will of My Father which is in
heaven. Many will say unto Me in that day, 'Lord, Lord,
have we not prophesied in Thy name, and in Thy name
have we cast out devils, and in Thy name done many wonderful works?' And then I will profess unto them, 'I
never knew you; depart from Me, ye that work iniquity.' " These men did not see so much worth in the waters of life as they did in iniquity. They did not prize

Christ's grace, His Spirit, the gospel and the promises thereof as much as works of iniquity. They would drink puddle water, poisonous water; they would not let go of their iniquity for Christ; yet these thought themselves Christians, thought themselves safe, happy, and blessed creatures. The five foolish virgins in Matthew 25 had lamps, but they had no oil in their lamps; they had none of this water of life; they had no grace; they had no Christ; they had none of the Spirit; they had none of the truths of God in their hearts. They thought that to profess Christ and the gospel was sufficient. They had lamps, but where was the oil? Where was the water of life? Where was grace? They had none of it.

2 Timothy 3:5 speaks of those who have a form of godliness, but deny the power thereof. They had a form; they came to the assemblies, just as you do, and sat there, heard the Word, professed Christ, seemed to be Christians, and, it may be, did something in their families. But they denied the power. They never had this willingness to see the excellence of the power of godliness. They never chose the power of godliness, never pursued the power of godliness.

Many in our day live in base and sinful ways, and yet think that they have the water of life, that they are living Christians; but it is with them as with the church of Sardis: they have a name as if they live, but they are dead indeed. What reviling is there of one another? What reproaching? What backbiting and slandering? What drunkenness, what whoredom, what oppression, what defrauding, what contention is there? Brother against brother, seeking to eat up one another and to undo one another, by ill language, seeking to gain advantage over one another, and yet these all desire to come to the Lord's Supper, whereas men who live in hatred and strife are murderers by Scriptural accounts.

It is a dreadful thing when those who are of the same family, flesh and blood, walk in those ways, and pretend that they are Christians. They would have the ordinances, but will not lay down their malice, vengefulness, and evil moods, not for Christ, not for waters of life, not for any of His ordinances. All are not true Christians who think they are; all have not tasted of the waters of life who think they have; all do not have grace who imagine that they do. The five foolish virgins got oil and came and knocked at the gate of heaven, but they were deceived. They did not have true oil, for they would have been let in then.

USE 2. This serves for reproof of many who say they would gladly have waters of life, who say they are willing and would fain have Christ, grace, and the Spirit. But it's evident that such is not the case, because they never prize them so as to see them as better than their earthly, sensual, and sinful enjoyments, than their outward estates, and whatever is dear unto them of that nature; they never make a real and actual claim of these waters, nor use the means to attain them. Corn, wine, and oil they prize, close with, make out after, and stir themselves so in the pursuit thereof that they hazard their souls eternally for them; but as for the waters of life, they care little for them. They have some sluggish desires after them, but no strong or lasting endeavors (Matthew 19:16–22; Luke 13:24).

Therefore it is not enough for men and women to say that they would have waters of life. There are many "wishers" and "woulders" in the world, but few truly and really will; they do not come to prize these waters, to choose them, and to use all the means available for them. They are not diligent to add grace to grace, to work out their salvation, to shake off security and slothfulness, and to put themselves forth as if it were a matter of life and death. Indeed, it is a matter of life and death to get these waters of life.

USE 3. If the willing man shall have the waters of life, then here God is excused and justified in the destruction of sinners. The Lord holds out waters of life freely. He says, "Whosoever will, whoseover is willing, let him take the waters of life. Let him live and be blessed, whoever is willing." Now if men perish, where is the fault? Who is to be blamed? God has provided Christ. He has provided the gospel and ordinances, provided His Spirit. He holds out the promises and says, "Whosoever will, whosoever is willing, come, come without money; here's water of life freely for you." Now if men perish, where's the fault? Revelation 3:20: "Behold, I stand at the door and knock; if any man will open the door, I will come in." And what if you will not open the door? If Christ beats down the house and the door and destroys him who is inside, who is at fault? The fault is yours, for you are not willing that Christ should come in.

Luke 19:27: "Those Mine enemies that would not that I should reign over them, bring hither and slay them before Me." God is saying, "Those enemies of Mine who would not have Me reign over them, tell them that I will cast out their enemies and reign sweetly and lovingly in them. I will do them good. I will save them, giving them waters of life and cordial comforts." Yet they will not come, and what then? "Bring those enemies and slay them before My face."

Matthew 23:37: "How often would I have gathered thee, even as a hen doth her chickens, *and ye would not.*" Christ is saying, "Had you been willing you would have eaten the fat and drunk the sweet wine; but you would not." What, then? "Now is your house left desolate." Man's destruction is of himself, and God is to be justified and cleared. He makes such tender offers of grace and mercy, and that freely. He comes and waits upon men and calls upon them, and yet they will not come. 2 Thessalonians 2:10–12: "Because they received not the love of the truth that they might be saved." Mark it: the truth was sent forth; the truth came, and the truth wooed them, but they would not receive the love of the truth. "But they received not the love of the truth that they might be saved; for this cause God shall send them strong delusions that they should believe a lie." And this is fulfilled exceedingly in our days, for the truth has come and knocked at the hearts of men and women, and it has not been received with the love of it. Therefore God has sent them a strong delusion so that they should believe a lie, "that they all might be damned who believed not the truth, but had pleasure in unrighteousness."

Men and women have pleasure in unrighteousness; therefore they will not receive the truths of God. And then God gives them over to strong delusions so that they might be damned. Had they received the truth, they would not have been damned nor had strong delusions. So that here God will be excused and justified in the damnation of sinners at last. John 3:19: "This is the condemnation, that light is come into the world, and men love darkness rather than light, because their deeds are evil." This will be their condemnation: they will shut their eyes against the light; they will not let truth enter; and, if they do, they withhold the truth in unrighteousness, and imprison the truth, as Herod did John.

USE 4. This serves for exhortation. "Whosoever will, let him take of the waters of life freely." Shall all who are willing have water of life freely? Then let us labor for this willingness. It is a matter of great concern; it concerns your souls and bodies for the present, and to all eternity, to see that there is this willingness in you, willingness to have waters of life. For all are not willing; nay, when it comes to the trial, hardly one in a hundred will be found really willing to have waters of life. Therefore give yourselves no rest night or day till you find a real willingness to have waters of life, to have Christ and the Spirit of Christ, to have grace, salvation, peace, and pardon for your souls. Give yourselves no rest, I say, till you find this willingness in you.

REASON 1. To excite you unto it, and then to show you how you may come to this willingness, first consider that you have a willingness toward other things, and that no willingness will do you any good without this one. Nay, your willingness toward other things may prejudice you, and *will* prejudice you unless you have this willingness. Men are willing to have honors, riches, and greatness in this world, willing to have all things about them in the best manner. What good will this do you unless you have a willingness to receive the waters of life? Riches will not deliver you in the day of wrath. There will be a day of wrath, and what will your riches, your honors, and all else do for you then? These will do nothing for you, but they may prejudice you. 1 Timothy 6:9–10: They that will be rich," and mark it, "they that *will* be rich," who have a willingness that way, who see an excellence in riches, who choose them and follow them—"they that will be rich fall into temptations, and a snare, and into many foolish and hurtful lusts, which drown men in destruction and perdition." Mark it, these prejudice you: "For the love of money is the root of all evil, which while some coveted after, they have erred from the faith and pierced themselves through with many sorrows."

When men have strong wills toward created things, they may prejudice themselves and undo soul and body. But if they have such a will to receive the water of life, that will be of great advantage to them. So "she that liveth in pleasure is dead while she liveth" (1 Timothy 5:6). Some people's wills carry them to pleasure—the pleasures of the body, carnal delights—and they are dead while they live. Have they waters of life? No, their wills have slain them. They are dead while they live. Ephesians 2:3: "Among whom we all had our conversation in time past in the lusts of the flesh, fulfilling the desires of the flesh," or "the wills of the flesh and of the mind." When we fulfill the wills of the flesh and of the mind, we are dead in sins and trespasses, children of wrath, enemies to God. So to have a will that prizes other things, that chooses and seeks after them, may damn you and undo you.

REASON 2. The second reason why you should labor to get this willingness is that this is what God requires, and that which He only requires; it is all that He does require. Under the covenant of works there was "Do this and live." But now the last motion that Christ made when He left the world and gave out the Scripture was this: "If any man has a will, if there is willingness in you to receive waters of life, that's the only thing I require, and all I require."

He does not require great matters at your hands. He does not say, "Give Me house and lands; give Me your shops and your wares; give Me your ships; give Me your limbs, your blood and your lives." No, He says, "If any man will, let Me have but willingness in you; this is all I require." Proverbs 23:26: "My son, give Me thy heart." What is His meaning? "Let Me but see a heart in you prizing, choosing, and pursuing the waters of life. That's all I require. My son, give Me your heart." He does not mean the piece of flesh in your body which you call your heart. But He would have you to have so much understanding as to see an excellence in Himself, His Son, His Spirit, His Word, and His grace, and then to choose the same, and to use the means to attain them. This is that which God requires, and all He requires. Shall the Lord only require your hearts, nothing but your hearts, and will you not study to have a heart willing to have God, to have waters of life?

REASON 3. Unless you are willing, you shall have no waters of life. Whosoever is willing, let him take the water of life. It is for him. God will never force you to it. If you lead a beast to drink, you do not force the beast to drink. And God will never force men. But if willingly they prize Christ, if they will choose Christ above all, if they will close with Him, if they will use the means that He has appointed to enjoy Him, Christ shall be their water of life; the Spirit shall be theirs. "Take, take immediately," He says, "take the water of life. It is for you and for none other."

By this time I think you are ready to say, "Oh, that we had this willingness in us. We hope we have it, or, if we do not, oh, that we had hearts willing now to prize Christ, to choose Christ, to close with Christ, His grace, His Spirit, His ways and ordinances. How shall we come by it?" I shall propound several considerations unto you whereby this willingness may be obtained.

CONSIDERATION 1. Consider your own condition. Let every man and woman, every son and servant seriously consider with themselves in what condition they are: "Were we not all lost in Adam? Are we not all under the law and the curse of the law? Are we not all enemies to God through wicked works in our minds? Have we not an abundance of guilt in our hearts and consciences? Are we not afraid of hell? If we should die, are we not afraid that we will be damned? Are we not helpless in ourselves, miserable creatures? Is not God just, holy, and righteous? Do not the greatest part of men go the broad way, and am I not in the broad way? Surely I am a wretched, miserable, lost, and undone creature. If any poor soul in the world has need of water of life, I am that creature."

For my own part, I speak freely here as in the presence of God. I know none of you who are greater sinners than myself; and none of you have greater need of the water of life than my own soul. Let us not deceive ourselves; we are all miserable and wretched creatures, and we all have need of the water of life, need of Christ, need of grace, need of the Spirit, need of promises, need of all.

When a man sits down and considers that he is in debt, owing much to many people, he realizes that he needs a friend to help him. This is our condition now. If you would but seriously consider, it would make you think, "Is there grace, mercy with God, redemption, salvation for sinners? Why not for me?" This would make you begin to have some willingness in you to have waters of life.

CONSIDERATION 2. Consider two things about Christ. First, consider the very end of Christ's incarnation, the end of His coming, the end of His being here in this world. Why did Christ come to earth? I will show you some places of Scripture.

Matthew 18:11: "For the Son of Man is come to save that which was lost." If anyone is a lost creature, Jesus Christ has come to save those who are lost. I hope, then, that He has come to save me, a lost creature. I am a lost sheep, a lost son, a lost goat. Surely if Christ came to save that which was lost, He came to save me.

It is a little fuller in Luke 19:10: "For the Son of Man is come to seek and to save that which was lost." He has come to seek that person out. He seeks the lost goat, the lost sheep. He seeks out lost sinners as He did the man at the pool of Bethesda: "Wilt thou be made whole?"

The man replied, "O Lord, I would fain be made whole, but I have none to help me."

"Then," said Christ, "be thou whole."

Now see what use Paul makes of it in 1 Timothy 1:15: "This is a faithful saying, and worthy of all acceptation, that Jesus Christ came into the world to save sinners, of whom I am chief."

O Lord, dost Thou come to save sinners? Here are glad tidings indeed, Lord! It's a faithful saying, worthy of all acceptation. You old ones should receive it; you young ones should receive it; you who are conceited in your own righteousness should receive it. Jesus Christ came to save sinners, whatever sinners they are: great sinners, old sinners who have lived many years in the height of wickedness, such as Paul—persecutors, injurious persons, and the like. If you seriously weigh this, it will make you willing to have these waters of life.

Second, consider how sweetly Christ invites you to take these waters of life. If an enemy would give you water when you were thirsty, would you not take it? But if the dearest friend you have in all the world should say, "O friend, you are thirsty; come, here's water, here's wine, here's milk, here's anything you would drink," you would take that well which was offered willingly.

Now, do you have a better friend in heaven and earth than Jesus Christ, who laid down His life and shed His blood for you? Christ said, "Whosoever will, let him come; take water, even water of life, poor soul. I have taken your nature upon Me. I have borne the wrath of God. I have satisfied the law. I have laid down My life. I come a-wooing you. I entreat you, do not damn yourself; do not throw yourself into hell. Poor soul, take hold of Me! Come, I'll lead you to the water of life. Come, I'll give you pardon, I'll give you peace, I'll give you My Spirit, I'll give you My blood. Why do you drink puddle water and poisoned water? Why do you not follow Me, but rather follow the devil, the beast, and your own lusts?" Thus the Lord Jesus Christ entreats us to take water of life.

In John 7:37 Christ stood up after a great feast and made a proclamation: "If any man thirst, let him come unto Me and drink." He was saying, "You have been drinking wine, water, and such things as do not quench the thirst of your souls. But if there is anyone among you who is thirsty for the waters of life, let him come unto Me. My arms are out; the waters are ready to give forth unto him; let him come and drink."

CONSIDERATION 3. Consider the promises, and in them consider three things:

First, consider the freeness of the promise: "Whosoever will, let him come and take of the water of life freely. I require no money, no qualifications or dispositions, but freely take them; only be willing to take them, and here they are." Revelation 21:6: "I will give unto him that is athirst (that is, who is willing) of the fountain of the water of life freely." If a man should freely say to all the poor people in a town, "Come, here's a pound apiece for everyone who will come," would not the poor come? Would not this beget a willingness in them? He does not say, "If you are thus clothed, if your hands and faces are clean, if you are finely dressed," no, but, "Let everyone come. Though you have leprous hands, scalded heads, lame legs, and are full of sores, come!" Thus it is with the Lord Jesus: His promise is free; whosoever will shall freely have the water of life.

Second, consider the sufficiency and fullness of the promise. If a promise is free, but does not have enough in it to relieve a man, then there is a problem. But there is a sufficiency and fullness in the promise. Romans 8:32: "He hath delivered up His Son for us all, and how shall He not with Him freely give us all things?" The promise has *all* things in it, all things needful for soul and body, for heaven and earth, for this life and the life to come; there's enough in the promise. Psalm 81:10: "Open thy mouth wide, and I will fill it." Let your desires be never so large, there's enough in the promise to satisfy your desires. Matthew 5:6: "Blessed are those that hunger and thirst, for they shall be satisifed." They shall have an abundance of satisfaction. John 10:10: "I am come that they might have life, and have it in more abundance." Would you have life, and be lively Christians? There's an abundance of life in Christ, an abundance of life in the Spirit and in the promise; there's enough to answer all your souls.

Third, consider the promise as being general. It is not limited to the Jew or Gentile, to one sort of men or women, but it is general: "whosoever will," whoever is willing. If it were made to rich men, poor men, learned men, noble men, wise men, or fools, then some question might be raised; but it's offered to all. If a state offers a pardon to all traitors, or all the delinquents therein, would not everyone come in and say, "I am a delinquent, but here's a pardon offered to me"? So every soul that is willing may come in and say, "Lord Jesus, Thou sayest, 'Whosoever will.' Lo, I am willing; let me have water of life." So the freeness, the fullness, and all the general offers of the promise unto all are special means to beget willingness in us to receive the water of life.

CONSIDERATION 4. Consider the excellence of these waters of life, the necessity of them, and the use of them. These waters of life have a greater excellence in them than anything you can imagine. There's nothing in all the world that is fit to be compared to the least drop of the water of life. All your gold, silver, diamonds, and pearls, all your gifts, parts, and things of that nature, are shadows in comparison to the waters of life. Christ, with all His merits, is water of life; the Spirit, with all His graces, is water of life; the gospel, with all its promises, is water of life. And you have great necessity of these. If you do not have them you will perish; you will die and be damned forever if you do not drink of these.

This water of life is of admirable use. Whosoever drinks of this water will be full of spirit and life, full of peace and comfort; they will be fitted for communion with God and man, for the service of heaven and earth. In John 7:37–39 Christ said, "If any man thirst, let him come unto Me and drink." It immediately follows, "This spake He of the Spirit, which they that believe on Him should receive. And out of his belly (he who believes) shall flow rivers of living water." He shall have living water to flow out of his belly, and will be useful so as to water others.

CONSIDERATION 5. Last, consider how easy that which the Lord requires at your hands is. The Lord requires no hard matters of you, only that whosoever will may take of the waters of life freely. The Lord might have put hard conditions and hard terms upon men and women. He might have done as Saul did with David in 1 Samuel 18:25: "Give me 100 foreskins of the Philistines, and thou shalt have Michal my daughter as your wife"; or as Caleb did when he said, "If any man will go and take Kiriath Sephar and subdue it, he shall have my daughter, Achsah" (Joshua 15:16). He might have put you upon it as he did the young man in Matthew 19:21: "Go and sell all that thou hast and follow Me, and thou shalt have waters of life." But He does not put you upon such things. He only says, "Whosoever will, let him come and drink of the waters of life." So it is easily received. Therefore, consider these things, and through the blessing of God they may prevail with your hearts to be more willing than ever to have water of life.

The next use is to let us see the infinite goodness of God, and His condescension toward poor creatures: that He who is greatness and glory, majesty and excellence, should condescend to us who are flesh and blood, who are corrupt, full of guilt, full of deformity, having no beauty, no excellence, no good in us; that God should condescend so far as that, upon our being willing, we should have waters of life. As was said before, He puts no hard terms upon us, but says, "Whosoever will, let him take of the waters of life." That is, "let him take Me for his portion; let him take My son. He shall be his righteousness. Let him take My Spirit; He shall be his sanctification. Let him take My Word; it shall be his light, his rule, and his comfort, and he shall be blessed here and hereafter."

Oh, the infinite goodness and condescension of God towards poor wretches such as we are! Had you seen Solomon in all his glory and royalty to have stooped this far to a poor woman, leprous and full of sores, having no friends to speak for her, and had you heard him say to her, "Come, manifest your willingness to have me, and I will take you into my house, wash you, make you my queen and make you happy," would this not have been a wonderful condescension from Solomon?

Thus it is with God. We were dirty and full of sores, with no friend to plead for us, but all was against us. We have no good or worth in us. Now Christ, the Prince of peace and life, comes and says, "Will you be saved, poor creatures? Will you be washed in My blood? Will you go along with Me? Will you be happy? Come, go along with Me. I will carry you to My Father. You shall sit upon a throne and live forever and enjoy God." Oh, the goodness and condescension of God to poor sinners!

Last, here is matter of comfort unto those who desire and thirst after waters of life. The doctrine said that those who are willing shall have waters of life. The text says that whoever will may take of the waters of life. Waters of life are prepared and reserved for those who are willing, for those who are thirsty. Therefore He says in Revelation 21:6: "If any man thirsts, He will give him of the fountain of the water of life freely." It may be that you thirst and are willing, but you still lack the waters of life. Is it so? Wait patiently; you shall have waters of life in due time, and they are worth waiting for. We can wait for a bottle of wine for two or three hours, and for a ship of wines for many months; and will you not wait for waters of life? Every promise is a tree of life: the fruit is growing, and when it's ripe you shall have it. Every promise is a bottle of wine, and when it pleases God He will uncork it and pour out the wine into your hearts. You shall have Christ and the Spirit to seal you up unto the day of redemption; you shall have the blood of Christ to wash you; you shall have God Himself, and all that is good; therefore wait.

Do but consider a little of the prodigal son in Luke 15:17–18: "And when he came to himself he said, 'How many hired servants of my father have bread enough, but I perish for hunger. I will arise and go to my father and say . . . .' And he arose and came to his father." Now mark it: here's the prodigal, and what does he say? "There's bread enough in my father's house; there's water of life in my father's house. Here I have nothing but stones; here there is nothing but swill for the swine. In my father's house there is bread." This shows that he prized it. "I will go eat of that bread." He chose it, and then he pursued it. "I will go." And so he went, making all the speed he could to get to his father's house and have it.

And was he long without it? See what follows: "And he arose and came to his father; but while he was a great way off, his father saw him, had compassion, ran and fell on his neck and kissed him. The son said, 'Father, I have sinned.' But the father saith to his servants, 'Bring forth the best robe, and put it on him, and put a ring on his hand, and shoes on his feet, and bring hither the fatted calf and kill it, and let us eat and be merry' " (Luke 15:20–23).

When you are this willing to have water of life, the Father sees you afar off and says, "There's one who is coming to Me; there is one who is coming for bread, for water of life." And what happens then? God will run and meet such a one. That one shall not be long without His water. God will kiss and embrace him, and give him water of life. He will give him wine, marrow, fatness, and all that is good. Therefore, be not discouraged, but move towards your Father's house, towards the waters of life, and it shall be brought forth unto you, and given to you in abundance.

Finis